GOING COMPREHENSIVE

Nick Moore. (Frank's son. 25:10:14)

GOING COMPREHENSIVE

or Unspoken Thoughts of a Deputy Head

published posthumously

L. F. Moore

Printed and bound in the UK by PublishPoint
from KnowledgePoint Limited, Reading

ISBN 9781904623045

Cover & Text Designed by PrePress-Solutions.com

CONTENTS

Chapter I

A Noble and Humane Objective

Large schools have their advantages. Expenditure per pupil on overheads is less than in smaller schools, and this makes it possible for Local Education Authorities to provide equipment on a lavish scale and a greater diversity of courses. This in turn is supposed to make possible the achievement of the goal of free, compulsory, universal, comprehensive education to enable us to erase from our system of schooling the handicaps of divisive and class-ridden selection, of insufficient and inefficient teaching. It is a noble and humane objective. It also makes economic sense, the sense of large-scale business enterprises. To many parents, teachers and politicians the issue of inequality of opportunity in our society is paramount in their consideration of all political and economic problems, so that for them the comprehensive school has become a panacea from the embrace of which there should be no escape or exclusion.

To the crusading zeal of these root and branch reformers are opposed the chronic anxieties of those to whom the wholesale destruction of ancient and revered institutions, or even of selective schools established less than a generation ago, appears less as a dream and more as a frightening chimera. In the world of educational discussions acceptance or rejection of the comprehensive school has become the shibboleth, and the arena of debate has become a battlefield across which the combatants view each other with increasing desperation. So much so that a commentator of the Times Educational Supplement made a plea to which this book may be regarded as a response: 'The voices which now need to be heard are those of the long-suffering, long or medium service professionals who know more about their schools than national or local politicians.'

Hazelwick, the comprehensive school in Crawley of which I was the Senior Academic Master and then for ten years the Deputy Head,

Philip

achieved a success and reputation which for many who observed it, including my Headmaster, Mr ~~Ronald~~ Keyte, clinched the argument that bigger meant better. A secondary modern school of nine hundred and fifty boys and girls, thirty of whom each year might at the end of six years achieve an average of three O levels, was transformed into a comprehensive of over seventeen hundred. The range of A level courses and the contingent of university entrants rivalled those of the grammar school on the other side of the town. When, as Senior Academic Master, I undertook the responsibility of transforming the work of a secondary modern into that of a comprehensive it would have done much to alleviate the stress and anxieties of the years immediately following re-organisation if it had been possible to foresee the success and acclaim that awaited us. The respect accorded by ambitious parents to a school that offers the prospect of places at Oxbridge to its brightest pupils was re-inforced by a reputation for all-round achievement that led to a demand for places in the school from parents living far outside the limits of the prescribed catchment area of our intake. The fact that this area comprised a group of neighbourhoods in a New Town with a rapidly expanding population helped to expedite the dissipation of the scepticism and hostility which greeted the initiation of the enterprise. Indeed, six years later, when the Deputy Director asked me to speak at a conference of head teachers on the problems of re-organisation, my satisfaction at being introduced as the man above all others in the county most qualified by my experience to address them on this momentous issue was tempered by the realisation that the public memory is short. Few besides the Headmaster and myself would find it easy to recall the overt animosity that all but overwhelmed us when our only credentials were our aspiration and our starting point a secondary modern school of equivocal reputation.

The circumstances in which I became involved at the comparatively late age of forty-five in what was virtually a pilot scheme for the Local Authority in developing comprehensive schools from secondary modern schools were curious, and in some respects not altogether edifying. My career as a schoolmaster had begun before the war in a Direct Grant grammar school. After the war and my demobilisation from the Army I made a brief excursion into politics which owed nothing to my interest in education but was really an extension of the political enthusiasm of my undergraduate days: I found that making political speeches was not difficult. In no time at all I was chosen as a delegate to a Labour Party conference. At the Conference I was chosen to move a composite resolution on behalf of a number of constituencies against the Party Executive. I made my speech and the resolution was carried. It attracted mention in reports of some of the national newspapers and letters of congratulation that should have encouraged me to persevere in politics like some of my contemporaries who subsequently achieved ministerial rank. Yet in the debates of that conference an intransigence amounting to what seemed to me close to megalomania so pervaded the speeches of constituency delegates that what might have been the beginning of a career was in effect the end of a youthful enthusiasm. I turned my back on these possibilities and returned to the humdrum work of teaching, poorly paid but safe.

It was at this same conference that I first was made aware of the Labour Party's interest in the idea of comprehensive schools, for at that time it had not yet become official policy and one of the highlights of the Conference was the rough ride given to the Minister of Education, Ellen Wilkinson. All of which was for me strangely devoid of interest. I did not immediately sever my links with the Labour Party. A few years later I joined an outing of a local party to visit one of the first large comprehensives to be built by the London County Council at Kidbrooke. Once again I experienced no stirring of interest. We were shown over the School by an official from the County Education Office. Halfway through our itinerary he halted our party to tell us that the School was so big that visitors like us often got lost. This information was imparted with what I can only describe as slobbering glee. Once again I sensed a whiff of megalomania and wondered if it militated against realism in all left-wing thinking about education. At that time I was also a member of the Fabian Society and attended their Summer Schools in Surrey. At these agreeable gatherings in the country it was possible to talk to old timers who reminisced about the pioneering days of the Social Democratic Federation whose dreams for the future were redolent of the world of William Morris. These veterans had gained an education based on intense private endeavour and the intimate communication of classes run by the Workers Educational Association. It was a far cry from the giant comprehensives of which the Labour Party had become enamoured and a paradox that so much individual striving should have culminated in an exercise in wholesale compulsion.

Most teachers who apply for posts in comprehensive schools do so for one of two reasons: either they are progressives, young men and women of high ideals who wish to help in the building of a more socially just and less class-ridden society, or they are teachers legitimately in pursuit of the more generous allowances paid to senior staff in big schools. My allowance as a deputy head was, for example, as large as that of a headmaster of a small school. In my case my application for the post of Senior Academic Master in a secondary modern about to become comprehensive was motivated by neither of these considerations. I noticed the advertisement for the job and thought no more about it. Then I received an anonymous message through the Headmaster of the grammar school at which I was Head of History and form master of the sixth that I ought to apply for the post of Senior Academic Master. The little that I knew about the school in question did not encourage me to apply and I dismissed the matter from my mind. Then I received a second message of similar import, again through my Headmaster. 'A little bird had told him.' I can think of no one less like a little bird than the large all persuading personality of the County Councillor, the educational pundit of the local Labour Party, whose game I was being chosen to play. His influence both at County Hall and in the local party exemplified the importance for success in public affairs of a mellifluous voice, the quiet assumption of omniscience, and a disarming equability of discourse. The confidence with which he delivered his opinions on all matters pertaining to education and a great deal else besides gave them the authority of unassailable verdicts, though, as I later discovered, he knew less about teaching than I did. Yet he probably surmised correctly that I needed more money. He may have also realised that at forty-five I was becoming bored with pushing grammar school pupils through GCE and that I was too old for a headship.

I had in fact been interviewed for a headship by the Deputy Director, with whom the County Councillor was in close and sympathetic communication, not long before I applied for what proved to be a very arduous post in the projected comprehensive. The headship in question was for a new grammar school and as such was one for which I regarded myself as fully qualified. I did not know, however, that the Authority already had plans to incorporate their new grammar school into a comprehensive school at a future date. The Deputy Director asked me what I thought about comprehensive schools. I replied perhaps a little too ingenuously but quite truthfully, that I thought, as I was being interviewed for a grammar school, that comprehensive schools were his problem, not mine. He concealed his reaction under his very thick glasses which at the time reminded me of an interrogator in a spy film. He did not, however, say 'We have other ways of making you talk,' but speedily brought the interview to a close. I like to think that my refusal to be drawn on the rights and wrongs of comprehensive schools was a spontaneous response born of intellectual integrity. I did not regard the opinion of anyone like myself who had not taught in either a secondary modern or a comprehensive school as worthy of consideration. The fact that the main ingredient of debates on educational issues is invariably the exchange of facile generalisations in no way diminishes my preference for conclusions based on a more intimate knowledge of the evidence. In justice to the Deputy Director I should add that it was he who later referred to me as the teacher 'most qualified to speak on the problems of re-organisation'.

If I had been asked for an opinion on the selection of pupils for grammar schools by means of the eleven plus examination I could have spoken without reservations. During my years as a teacher in grammar schools I had been shocked by the tensions inflicted on children, sometimes by over-anxious parents on children still in the infant stage. As the father of three children I did not wholly escape from speculating on the consequences of rejection at eleven plus. In the event, two of them passed into grammar schools without difficulty and the third was a beneficiary of the comprehensive system. Though I never sank to the level of cajolery or the corruption of bribery by rewards of bicycles and the like, I understood the intensity of the anxiety that underlay these practices when I supervised eleven plus exams and witnessed the nail biting, the precipitate rush for the lavatories. My faith in the infallibility of selection by compulsory examination was also undermined by having to teach those boys who quickly demonstrated their unsuitability for a grammar school course by gravitating to the 'C' stream. Although I subsequently developed firm conclusions about the altogether different tensions endemic in comprehensive schools nothing in my experience has caused me to revise my view of the iniquity of selection or rejection at eleven plus by examination. The very human predilection for simplifying complex questions has to my mind bedevilled and nullified most public discussion of the comprehensive school debate. This is true even among groups with pretensions to intellectual status. After the success of the enterprise in which I became so deeply involved was assured, both the Headmaster and I were much in demand as speakers on 'comprehensiveness', a role into which he entered with much less trepidation than I did. I soon discovered that audiences had a marked preference for hearing what they already believed. According to the theorists the comprehensive school was to be justified primarily as the agency for abolishing social and class distinctions. My testimony that the main benefit of a successful comprehensive was academic rather then social and derived from the wider application of a higher and more demanding standard of teaching was not always well received. This was most apparent when I spoke at branch meetings of the Fabians. When I averred that there was little evidence that a quite remarkable improvement in both work and recreational activities was reflected in a comparable diminution of social affiliations I sensed an unreasoning rejection of what I knew to be true as a matter of proven fact. On one occasion my Fabians audience lost all interest in my discourse and fell to arguing among themselves, leaving me to make an unceremonious departure without formalities. They were even less pleased when I adduced evidence that the most effective and simplest device for alleviating the tensions between dissimilar social groups was an intransigent adherence to a school uniform. Such heresies, however, presented no difficulty to parents whose concern was less with a blue-print for a new society than for the advantages supposedly enjoyed by boys and girls at grammar schools.

In his autobiography Lord Wigg, a peer of unimpeachable working-class origins and Labour Party affiliations, makes the following judgement: 'all educational opportunity should be based on the principle of universality,' and, in the same paragraph, 'the soundest feature of the English schooling system is the Grammar School.' It was with similar convictions that I undertook the task of organising the work of a comprehensive school. Shortly before I left the Grammar School to take up this task of superimposing grammar school attainments on a secondary modern school I received a sombre warning from a colleague. He was a teacher of unusual qualifications and experience in that he was a teacher of Metalwork who also taught Latin. He thus possessed a rare knowledge of the extremes of abilities of both pupils and teachers in the two types of schools. His verdict on my chances of success in my new role was succinct. 'What you are going to try and do is impossible.' No one, from Education Officers and HM Inspectors downwards, apart from my Latin-Metalwork friend, ever made reference to this root problem of English secondary schooling, the existence of two disparate bodies of teachers, divided not only by differing qualifications and training but even more by the priorities of the schools in which they worked. My post of Senior Academic Master was not to be found in the established hierarchy of secondary schools. It was in my case an ad hoc creation tacitly adopted to strengthen the hand of a non-graduate secondary modern headmaster whose speciality always remained a matter for speculation but which was generally believed to be Woodwork. As a teacher whose whole career had hitherto been in grammar schools, I was about to discover the extent and significance of this gulf in what I had believed to be a profession. Every public utterance in which Ministers of Education refer to teachers as if they were a body of men and women with common standards and assumptions reflects either culpable ignorance or calculated chicanery.

My twelve years, ten of them as a deputy head, of joint endeavour with a secondary modern headmaster was an experiment which was to vindicate Lord Wigg's verdict, despite the dichotomy. It was also to disprove the pessimism of my Latin-Metalwork colleague, but only just. The Deputy Director once described my Headmaster, with whom he had tied me into a relationship of inescapable and sometimes abrasive interdependence, as a 'very modern' secondary modern headmaster. By this he meant that by training and by temperament the Headmaster was quintessentially a product of the immediately postwar period of secondary schooling, the years in which the insistent and inflexible teaching of the elementary schools was replaced by a freedom from defined objectives, the main result of which was a plethora of experiments and an instability of practice wholly inimical to the self-discipline upon which professional standards must be based. The conjunction of two men, each epitomising the divergent assumptions of the two main sectors of our system of secondary schools, was bound to place an almost intolerable strain on both of us. We taught each other a great deal. I learnt later from the headmaster of a grammar school on the far side of the county that my headmaster was transformed from being an excoriating critic of grammar school teachers into an equable colleague on various committees where his status as the headmaster of a reputable comprehensive made him very much persona grata among those against whom he was wont to inveigh. As far as I am aware I emerged from our partnership with my convictions intact and vindicated. From mutual incomprehension we both progressed to concession or compromise. The ambiguous terms of my appointment had tacitly conferred on me a measure of autonomy which I never surrendered, a truly unique relationship between a headmaster and his deputy, the character of which was never fully understood except by the County Councillor from whose machinations it emerged, and by a few colleagues of grammar school origin whose work brought them into intimate contact with both the Headmaster and myself. As the subordinate partner I had to develop a tact and discretion with which to compensate for the intransigence of my professional beliefs. What it cost me to do so was a slow declension in my health. The health of my Headmaster appeared to improve.

Not long before I resigned my post as deputy head there occurred an incident in the Headmaster's study which for me highlighted our peculiar relationship. The Headmaster was in conference with the local HM Inspector about an extension to the School buildings. It was not usual for me to be present at such communings but to be available to provide detailed information. On this occasion I was present for the whole afternoon. My contribution was to advise which of the academic departments were most in need of extra accommodation. It so happened that there was a strong case for an extra room equipped for Technical Drawing. This having been accepted, I found it necessary to interpose repeatedly in order to direct the discussion towards the consideration of the consequences of this decision. What department, for example, was to be reduced by one teacher if we appointed another Technical Drawing teacher to occupy the new room? What extra craft room and staffing would we require for the girls of those classes from which the boys would be timetabled for lessons in the new Technical Drawing room? In short I urged consideration of the chain reaction of curricular adjustments that would follow from the provision of an extra room. At the close of our discussion Her Majesty's Inspector expressed satisfaction at the usefulness of our uninhibited exchanges. It seemed that he had witnessed something unusual. This surprised me so much that I asked him whether, in his experience, it was unusual for headmasters to involve their deputies in impromptu deliberations. It was, I was told, most unusual. I then asked the Inspector whether he thought most deputies tended to become sycophantic. He paused and thought for a while before replying. 'Yes,' he said.

The grim wariness with which a teacher approaches the interview for what may prove to be his last appointment provides a stark contrast to the gay insouciance with which so many of us entered teaching. My first post was at a Direct Grant school in Newcastle-upon-Tyne. It was offered me by the Headmaster after what seemed to me a most superficial interview, the main point of which was to allay his concern that I should teach history without making my lessons the means of indoctrinating the boys with communist ideas. The casualness of his offer was matched by the alacrity of my acceptance, despite the fact that I knew nothing about the School or the place, which was three hundred miles from home. Nowadays the chronic shortage of teachers affords a greater exercise of discrimination to youngsters who have to think more about mortgages than the fine points of distinction between one school and another. Generally speaking it remains true, however, that it needs the sobering experience of years of teaching to induce the circumspection and suspicion with which one looks at the place in which to serve the last stretch.

Before attending the interview for a Senior Academic Master I drove across the town for a discreet look at the boys and girls as they emerged from the School at four o'clock. I noticed a prevailing hastiness in their dispersal, a pell mell escape from the campus, and I was uneasy. I failed to recall the psychological maxim that intuitions which run counter to self interest should be treated with respect, and I dismissed my misgivings as irrational. It was not long afterwards, when during my first year I encountered the full force of the suspicion of the parents who feared having to send their children to a new comprehensive or perhaps to an old secondary modern school, that I learned that the impression made by pupils going to and from a school was for many parents the paramount circumstance determining their attitude to a school. I am aware that the avant garde among educationists tend to discount such manifestations of parental prejudice, especially if it can by dismissed as middle class or bourgeois. Yet my sympathies in this matter are with the parents. I have learned that when an apparent prejudice is deeply rooted, as was the case of parents who lived near the secondary modern school and found what they saw of it difficult to reconcile with the promise of grammar school standards to follow from re-organisation, it is worthy of respect even if based on considerations not immediately discernible.

In this connection I am reminded of an incident in which I was involved when I was eight years old. It occurred at the end of a football match between the boys of what in the nineteen twenties were called elementary schools, of Beckenham and Sidcup. Such fixtures were in those days rare and memorable events. Otherwise I do not think I would have been among the children watching the game, for I have never been deeply stirred by football although I played it at school and in the street until introduced to the thrills of rugger at the age of sixteen. I remember nothing of this childhood event except the brightness of the jerseys worn by the players and what happened at the end of the game. There must, I suppose, have been some cause of resentment on the part of the home supporters, though what it was remained beyond my childish comprehension. All I can remember is that as soon as the final whistle was blown I was in the thick of a howling mob in noisy chase of the Sidcup team who ran in flight from the field. We chased them up the road until they disappeared to the sanctuary of a local school. This is the only occasion in my life, if my memory is not at fault, when I was swept into total irrationality by the exhilaration of mob emotion. I am grateful for the recollection. The innocence of children in the mass, bereft of adult supervision, is an assumption underlying much contemporary writing about schools with which I am much out of sympathy. Parents who look askance at unruliness when a school disperses could be wiser than many of the self-styled educationists.

My interview for the post of academic supreme in the new comprehensive was in February 1960. The making or breaking of teachers by appointing committees is a feature of English education which inspires little confidence among teachers. I was one of those who enjoyed being interviewed, though, as I was to learn later when as a deputy head I became privy to the confidential parts of the appointing procedure, this was a relatively unimportant consideration. Of one thing I became convinced. The type of governor appointed by the left-wing party hacks who soon secured control of the New Town is easily impressed by plausible, facile, high-minded sentiments. The paranoia which underlies so much of their politics predisposes them to favour an attitude of undiscriminating benevolence towards children. Young men who could convey by their responses or demeanour that they shared this conviction that there was nothing in the running of a school that could not be solved by a sympathetic chat, a kindly word and a smile could wipe the floor with older and wiser professionals. A good profile was an advantage, and, coupled with these sentiments, a public school background was no disadvantage in a Labour controlled town.

Fortunately for me I was not being interviewed for a headship. Nor were the Governors so ingenuous as they later became. As a teacher I had been self critical and a perfectionist. It was not cynicism but a constant brooding about my job that engendered convictions which would not have endeared me to facile optimists. The key fact to success in teaching children of secondary school age is never to forget that they turn up to lessons because they have to. You could sugar this pill by every conceivable stratagem but to embrace illusions in contradiction of this truth was the short way to disaster. For most children, most of the time, the most welcome part of a lesson was the sound of the bell at the end of it. My youngest child, the one who enjoyed school most, re-inforced my suspicion on this point when he was interviewed for admission to his comprehensive school, a progressive and child-centred institution. When asked at the conclusion of his interview whether there was any question he would like to ask, 'Yes,' he sternly replied. 'What time do you finish?' It does not help a teacher to gain promotion, when confronted by trendy governors, to reveal too much awareness of the realities of the job.

In my experience the old-fashioned type of governor, the retired public servant or person of independent means who wished to be of use to the community, was preferable to the politically appointed doctrinaire whose concern for the welfare of humanity was never matched by any concern for the individual teacher. I remember my first interview in the New Town when I was appointed to the staff of the Grammar School. At that time the retired colonel and his like had not yet been displaced by nominees from the Trades Council. To the consternation of the Education Officer who had conducted applicants on a tour of the New Town I expressed reluctance at this opportunity to embrace a life among the proletariat. I was not sure that my family would regard the move to a working class milieu as a change for the better. The governors were not only sympathetic but went to the trouble of showing me the older part of the town. I also learned from them that the Education Officer lived in an architect-designed house in what estate agents would describe as a desirable residential area.

My appointment as Senior Academic Master at the new comprehensive was not typical. Very understandably the Governors interrupted their terms of reference in a narrow sense of the word 'academic' and made no attempt to investigate my attitude to children. What is more surprising they did not question me on my views about comprehensive schools. It might be supposed that their selection was influenced by the fact that I was already known to half of them. This was not the case, as I learned from recent conversations about these now almost forgotten events with those who were present. The Headmaster for one did not favour my appointment. I certainly would not have guessed it from the warmth of his welcome when I joined him.

The attempts to determine my fitness for a strictly academic role were cursory and far less searching than the questions I used to put to mere beginners when I later had to assist the Headmaster at making appointments. Nothing was asked about teaching techniques, the vexed problems of marking, homework, examinations, streaming, grades, reports, or timetabling. For this I was grateful. Any attempt to communicate on these matters would probably have resulted in misunderstanding. Yet it is in this almost complete inability of Governors to discuss such fundamental aspects of teaching that the great weakness of our system lies. Their preference for questions about sentiments governing relationships in a school is a reflection of the amateurism that bedevils English schooling from top to bottom. No advantage accrues to the teacher who achieves sufficient detachment and objectivity to analyse and appraise his own performance. Teaching techniques remain too much a matter of temperament, custom and habit, changing only slowly if at all in response to new ideas.

I remember being asked two questions pertinent to the appointment. How many subjects should be taken at GCE O level? How many subjects should be taken before the introduction of options? It so happened that I had arrived at firm conclusions on both these questions. The practice of overloading the timetable of third formers with as many as thirteen subjects was one with which I was familiar. The idea behind it is to introduce children to as many subjects as possible before a final choice of subjects for GCE. I had long regarded it as a wasteful and inefficient way of diagnosing aptitudes. It is a matter of common knowledge that third year pupils are at the lowest ebb of their interest in work or study of any sort. Those who in earlier years had been highly motivated by a desire to win approval from teachers ceased to be so. At the same time few third formers become mature enough to be affected by considerations of future careers. The third year is essentially an interlude of skimped homework, of working to rule. I adumbrated these views to the Governors who did not demur. Yet the significance and irony of this exchange lay in the fact that when I came to establish the curriculum of the School I adopted the very ideas that I had so unambiguously repudiated. Neither the Governors or I had reckoned with the weight of parental opinion in this matter which proved to favour a postponement of options and specialisation for as long as possible.

If I had to put my finger on the prime circumstance that determined the ultimate success and character of the School, I would indicate the policy upon which the Headmaster and myself remained consistently agreed, of deference to articulate parental pressure. Unlike those who earn their keep in the uplands of the education system, in Institutes and Colleges of Education, Headmasters find it impossible to ignore the fact that children have parents, even if they do not always go so far as I did in acknowledging the sovereignty of parental right, or the primacy of the family among the institutions upon which a civilisation is based. Good schools may at best mitigate the defects of a bad home. They can never be so good as to substitute for a good home. In so far as I experience antipathy to the more extravagant theories emanating from teacher training establishments it is a reflection of the unfortunate impression made on me at seminars, conferences and the like sponsored by these pundits. The patronising attitude to parents which I encountered on these occasions seemed to me inexcusable and repellent. The sincerity of my own professional protestations would, I hope, not be found wanting when tested by reference to my practices as a parent. The occupation of teaching other people's children does not confer overriding rights to determine their future. I am not sure that it even confers a superiority of insight.

I think I can come clean, as they say, on this issue. It was never known to my employers, nor do I think it was any of their business, that I went so far in the case of my eldest child to investigate the possibilities of withdrawing her from junior school and teaching her myself at home. I can remember the visit by one of His Majesty's Inspectors to certify my fitness for this task, but I cannot remember why I decided not to go through with it. The nature of her difficulties was not, I regret to say, unusual. Unhappiness at school of more than a temporary nature ought not to be accepted. It may, of course, be caused by and reflect a greater unhappiness at home, in which case the problem is indeed intractable. What goaded me to action was the ineptitude of a teacher whose innate limitations were made less acceptable by a constant resort to that most unprofessional of habits, sarcasm at children's expense. I must not fall into the deplorable fallacy of talking about children's rights. I am, however, convinced empirically that a happy childhood is the first prerequisite of strength in maturity, of broad shoulders capable of carrying with cheerfulness the stresses of adult life. For this reason I am totally out of sympathy with the practice so prevalent among teachers at the present time of trying to induce in children what is euphemistically called a sense of responsibility in increasingly permissive situations, but which in my view is a dissemination of the anxieties of guilt feelings and an infection with adult neuroses.

This is perhaps the point at which to underline my affiliations and convictions by revealing another thing which was never known to my colleagues, let alone my employers. When I read in the papers of the case of a Mrs Baker in Norfolk who was prepared to go to prison rather than send her children to a school she deemed unsuitable, and who resolved to undertake their education at home, I wrote letters to various members of Parliament who were reputed to have a concern for the liberty of the individual. None was moved by the plight of Mrs Baker, but happily she succeeded in her enterprise without their help. As for me I cite the episode as evidence that, quite apart from the question of the liberties of the individual, I believe many of our schools are places where children encounter less instruction than corruption. This will remain so until teaching ceases to be the refuge of the half-educated in search of security and a shred of gentility.

It would have been an event breaking the bounds of my credulity if any interviewing committee had ever elicited from me a hint of these opinions. Having regard to the limited view the Governors took of the responsibilities I was about to undertake, it was not unreasonable of them to confine their enquiries to the obvious. In any case I had little more insight than they had into the intractable nature and extent of the problems of re-organisation. To effect a change in the academic performance of a school is not a mere matter of devising new curricula. It involves the conversion of everyone from the Headmaster downwards to a new scale of priorities and pre-occupations. I was to meet many sanguine headmasters and headmistresses in the next few years among the visitors to the School who cheerfully outlined their draft schemes for re-organisation. No doubt they are wiser now. It is not that easy.

At the time of my interview the parents of the neighbourhoods to be served by the new comprehensive had not been involved. Indeed, as later became only too apparent, there was no intention of involving them more than was unavoidable. The statutory obligations to promulgate the change of status in the School as set down in the Education Act of 1944 were deemed not to apply. As events unfolded this was a view of the situation which, as far as I could see, became less and less tenable. For the present, however, all that was happening was that a secondary modern school, albeit a very secondary 'modern' secondary school, was being re-organised to cater for the admission of children of grammar school ability. The parents of such children had as yet no reason to believe that anything was afoot to deprive them of their places at the Grammar School. No notices of change ever appeared. Though the funds for building a fine new block for an Upper School had already been voted, as I discovered from my researches through the minutes of the County Council, no report of this appeared in the local press. Yet within less than a decade this furtive re-organisation had achieved such dramatic success that head teachers and their deputies were being despatched by County Hall to see what great things could be done by going comprehensive. The brinkmanship with which the County pioneered its first re-organisation might have commanded admiration had it not been for the supine and continuing ignorance evinced by Education Officers of the human cost of the operation. The whole thing was in fact a remarkable tour de force. As such it should have been discounted. Any institutions which only function successfully when staffed by men or women of exceptional ability and dedication, and which founder and fail when run by mediocrities, do not provide models for general adoption.

When I reached home after the interview I told my wife that I had been appointed. We were both subdued by apprehension of the unknown. I reclined wearily on our well-worn sofa. Like two desperate characters in a Kingsley Amis novel we consoled ourselves with a bottle of cheap Spanish wine. At least the weeks of perplexity and indecision were at an end.

What, I ask myself, was the best job I ever had? When I was twenty-eight I was Gunnery Officer on Britain's largest refrigerator ship, zig-zagging to and from New Zealand with London's butter ration. It was a wonderful experience, being one's own boss. I was able to give full rein to my perfectionism without interference from anyone. I didn't need to smoke or drink, not even with whisky and gin at tuppence halfpenny a time. If there was to be any shooting we had to fire first and not miss. I trained those gunners day after day. At first they hated it. They had looked forward to putting their feet up and getting out the cards when they were not on watch looking for submarine periscopes. Then they became so good that they became proud of it and hoped I would be with them on the next trip. The routine, however, did not allow this and I returned to gunnery instruction. The War Office noticed my report and in one of their circulars commented on what could be done by training at sea in merchant ships by a determined officer. I was at my best when completely in charge. This was another thing that never came out at interviews.

CHAPTER II

THE CULT OF EDUCATION

A week after my interview I had my first consultation with my future headmaster. He invited me to an informal evening at his house. Aided by interpositions from his deputy he unfolded for me the incredible organisation of an eight-form-entry secondary modern school. Although later, when I was deputy head, it became a twelve-form-entry comprehensive, it was so much bigger than any grammar school I had known that I quickly realised I was moving into a totally unfamiliar environment. This was my initiation into the way 'the other half' lived. I was given a partial intimation of the immense but unmentionable divide in English state secondary schooling. There has doubtless been, since then, an increasing number of grammar school teachers who have found themselves in a minority in a secondary modern school. Let them be judges of my bewilderment as I learned about the staff organisation of a large secondary modern school, with its carefully graded hierarchy of Heads of Schools, Tutor Administrators, Heads of Departments, Assistant Heads of Departments, and Teachers in Charge of this and that. What impressed me and surprised me most was the unmistakeable importance of these gradations. Unlike the predominantly graduate world of grammar schools, where headmasters were primus inter pares and not far removed from the status or sheltered from the freely expressed views of independently minded subordinates, the secondary modern school appeared to me as a place where the headmaster was a long way removed from this colleagues at the bottom of the pile. Indeed, one of the problems I later encountered as deputy head was the inability of young members of staff to think of me, let alone their headmaster, as a colleague. What also struck me as strange and not immediately explicable was the number of teachers in this hierarchy who received 'special responsibility allowances' for functions unrelated to teaching. Although this feature of secondary school organisation may have spread to some grammar schools in the past decade, I was of the generation of whom some part in discharging the various non-teaching chores of a grammar school was taken for granted without consideration of payment.

I well remember the introduction of special-responsibility allowances at the grammar school in which I was working immediately after the War. The Headmaster came into the staff room and announced with obvious embarrassment and perplexity that he was obliged to designate a number of us as deserving of special responsibility allowances. The staff immediately rejoined, and the headmaster agreed, that we were all very responsible men. After a brief discussion it was agreed that those of us with the largest tax allowances in respect of dependants or mortgages should be nominated to take advantage of this new source of emolument. Our contempt for this disastrous innovation which was to destroy completely the stability of school staffing, leading eventually to a scandalous and crippling turnover of teachers hunting for promotion and extra cash, continued for some years after its inception. I was responsible for a resolution at a branch meeting of the Assistant Masters Association that the new allowance system should be rescinded. Although it was defeated I suspect that this was so because the new system had already divided the interests of the older men from the younger. Yet as late as 1960 the post-war divide and rule pay structure had not so far resulted in deferential attitudes or awareness of place in grammar school staff rooms. It came as a surprise to me to discover how much it was an accepted feature of life in my new school.

My new Headmaster, on the other hand, was equally unfamiliar with the professional egalitarianism of the grammar school. Unlike me he was not surprised or shocked when one of my new colleagues deemed it necessary to write a note asking permission to speak with me. This was only one of many features of the dissimilarity between the two sectors of the secondary system. This first encounter was only an initiation. When we began to work together there were moments of total mutual incomprehension, the source of which must be traced back to the day on which some sixth formers leave school for university and a teaching career, and some leave for Colleges of Education in which, so it is alleged, they receive a training more closely related to teaching than those who graduate. My experience led me to place a very low value on the training for teachers for secondary schools in Colleges of Education.

My immediate reaction to the exposition by the Headmaster of the staffing of his school was confusion and curiosity. The pretentiousness of the titles that featured in his hierarchy made me wonder whether any senior staff were at all involved in the basic business of teaching. Although I was assured that all the staff had teaching timetables I was left with an overwhelming impression that a pre-occupation with administration was going to prove a drain on teachers' energies and act as a circumstance inimical to high academic standards. I was not wrong. It took at least three years to evolve and establish a routine of academic events, such as examinations, promotions meetings and the like, which were so arranged as to cause as little interruption to the timetable as possible. The steady rise in the School's academic achievements, an increase of as much as eleven hundred per cent in the case of O level passes, stemmed largely from the primacy won for adherence to the teaching timetable and the recruitment of teachers who resented rather than welcomed interruption to lessons. I never entirely gained the acceptance of the Headmaster to this view of things and he continued to summon members of his former secondary modern staff to his study even though this caused them to leave their classes unattended. On the other hand he respected not only my attitude but that of other ex-grammar-school men who later joined the staff in senior posts such as Head of Upper School. I very much appreciated the courtesy he accorded me of sending for me to go to his study when I 'had finished teaching'. It must have often called for great forbearance on his part, for he was an impulsive and energetic man who was temperamentally averse to working in conference with others.

The feature of secondary modern schooling which I never came to accept or to eliminate from the School when it became comprehensive was the predilection for conferences, discussion, short courses, all of which took place in school time and caused constant interruption to teaching. The cult of education has produced a lot of jobs for people who want to cash in on it without actually having to teach. I use the term 'cult' to indicate a religious attitude unsupported by any belief in the supernatural, but one which sustains a wholly irrational degree of expectation. As a comprehensive deputy head I was brought into contact with many enthusiasts for education who evinced this tendency to regard it as some sort of religion. Among its less agreeable manifestations was an insatiable proclivity for seeking enlightenment through organised discussions, a sort of substitute for prayer meetings. In my lifelong habit of reading history I have not come upon many instances of great advances which were not the fruit of the endeavours of highly gifted individuals rather than discussion groups. Perhaps the Authorised Version and the American Constitution are the most obvious exceptions. Unfortunately this contemporary addiction for discussion has even found its way on to the teaching timetables of large schools where it erodes the sense of purpose of both teachers and learners, and gives too much play to the idiosyncrasies of the former. I found the secondary modern tradition a fertile soil for the propagandists among educationists, and a great aid to the empire-building activities of conference organisers. All the inducements of educationists to lure teachers away from teaching, to conferences and courses of ephemeral consequence, developed in me an intense hostility to the very word 'educationists'. Not the least objectionable feature of these pseudo-professional exercises was their inconclusiveness. Education appears to me more and more as a subject in which it is unseemly to the point of obscenity to arrive at firm conclusions. For this reason I came to prefer to direct the attention of student teachers allocated to me for supervision to problems of imparting knowledge, overcoming ignorance, adjusting to limitations of intelligence, even to a consideration of that most desirable but elusive quality, a sense of responsibility. I found I could do very well without reference to 'education', and I still feel demeaned if anyone refers to me as an educationist. And it doesn't impress me that you can now get a degree in it. Indeed, in my casual radio listening I have heard discussions on Open University programmes which have strengthened my antipathy.

My previous career as a grammar school teacher had never been interrupted by the spurious pretensions of the conference organisers. We were never asked to abandon lessons or diminish the syllabus to make time to go and listen to some non-teaching expert expounding the latest emanation from an ivory tower. This indifference of grammar school teachers to the torrent of specious wisdom from self-appointed pundits was a trait that differentiated them so markedly from secondary modern teachers. I first encountered this disparity while I was still a grammar school teacher and went to a conference organised by the National Union of Teachers. As they had hired the grammar school in which I worked for part of their conference I decided to put in an appearance as a matter of courtesy. I chose to attend a lecture on the teaching of History. My dismay at the rigmarole of recommended gimmicks for use in the classroom was made all the more acute by the fervour with which the audience of teachers scribbled down as much as they could of this charlatanic discourse. This happened before I 'went comprehensive' and I might be excused for thinking that some progress has since occurred towards a greater sophistication among teachers in general. Yet it was after my retirement that I talked with a headmaster of a grammar school of great reputation whose school had just been combined with a neighbouring secondary modern to form a comprehensive. He imparted in tones of incredulity and perplexity his astonishment at the discrepancies in the attitudes of the two sections of his new staff. I do not know whether he stayed in this post long enough to accustom himself to the problem or to achieve a synthesis of professional practice. I felt sorry for him and angry with the culpable ineptitude of the administrators to whom this aspect of re-organisation remained a matter of no consequence. This particular headmaster had been one of those despatched by the County to admire the success of our pioneering enterprise in re-organisation in the New Town. On that occasion, as on all similar visitations, professional restraint prevented the discussion of what happens when you have to operate as though teachers were a homogenous profession.

Another misconception which my Headmaster and I had to clear up in the early stages of our co-operation was the view that teachers in grammar schools have an easier job than teachers in secondary modern schools. I might have shared this view had I not spent a term during which I started my work in the secondary modern more or less as an observer prior to the actual re-organisation while still driving to and from my previous school to finish my syllabus with the classes about to take O level and A level for which I had been responsible. The secondary modern teachers generally speaking, and with notable exceptions, worked much shorter hours than those at the Grammar School. It was almost always possible for me to return to the Grammar School after four o'clock and be sure of finding the whole staff still at work of some sort, usually marking, for the next hour or so. This was not the case at the secondary modern, though it became much more true of the latter after it had become comprehensive. The truth is that teaching in a grammar school is for most graduates a more congenial occupation conducive to a greater commitment than most secondary modern teaching. The most marked exception to this generalisation was the dedication of some of the remedial teachers who later came to the comprehensive. As a grammar school teacher I had been primarily concerned with sixth form work and university entrance. When I became deputy head of the comprehensive I quickly decided that I had to timetable myself with what were rightly regarded as the most difficult, the below average classes containing a high proportion of fourth year leavers. Taking my twelve years as a Senior Academic Master and Deputy Head in a comprehensive as a whole, I found from looking over my timetables that I spent seventy-five per cent of my teaching time with these less than average ability classes. I discovered that teaching of this category, although it called for greater care and skill in the seemingly casual exchanges with pupils who appeared to me slightly paranoic towards teachers, was a much less tiring job than teaching high-ability classes. The latter produced such a mass of work. If one did the job properly it all had to be marked with the same precision and in the same detail as was expected of the paid external examiners who would be the final arbiters of these children's efforts. The pace of work, whatever the technique, was in the case of the lower-ability classes so much slower and productive of correspondingly smaller output that individual attention could be given with much less stress.

When I look back and try to make a dispassionate assessment of what I learned as a teacher in a comprehensive school I have to claim that I learned a great deal, particularly from my work with the less intelligent classes. I will not call them Newsom children, for I abhor the concept and the Report which gave it currency. I learned a flexibility in choice of material and a greater care in the choice of vocabulary. Yet I do not think I would have learned nearly as much if I had lowered my standards in respect of the strict adherence to a detailed syllabus and the maintenance of an intensity of work which I owed to my many years in grammar schools. I never learnt the taste for 'mucking about' as substitute for teaching. My immediate impressions of secondary modern schools may have been narrowly based, but nothing that I heard from others like me who 'went comprehensive' caused me to revise my judgement.

My last day as a grammar schoolmaster was marked by appropriate formalities. Both in the end-of-term assembly and in the staff-room presentations the Headmaster of the Grammar School made a speech about my professional qualities that evoked such a volume of applause that I was moved and experienced a lump in my throat. I confess this reluctantly. In my view children are called upon to applaud platform sentiments with a degree of frequency that would not be tolerated in any adult institution.

The interesting sequel to this farewell eulogy was not revealed to me until much later. Although I was forty-five years old I still made the occasional application for a headship, and invariably gave the name of the gentleman who had praised me so unreservedly as one of my referees. A year or so later I received a cryptic letter from a colleague who had become a headmaster. His letter consisted of a brief warning against giving the name of my grammar school headmaster and attaching too much importance to a platform utterance. I am not sure to this day whether this advice was well founded. Yet it prompts the reflection that confidential references, as distinct from open testimonials, are the key to promotion in the state system. It surprises me that the teachers' unions have not made it a major item in their objectives to rid teachers of the incubus of 'the confidential'. This lukewarmness is perhaps understandable in the case of The National Union of Teachers in which headmasters play such a dominant part. Headmasters are understandably reluctant to forego such a useful device in the discharge of their responsibilities for appointing staff. The eye of a needle through which a good man must pass is thus the unqualified approval of his headmaster or, as I dare say, his headmaster's wife. This consideration is a great disincentive to the exercise of initiative, the more so the nearer one is to the boss in the school hierarchy. A young teacher in a large comprehensive can allow himself all manner of idiosyncratic foibles to enliven his lessons. His remoteness from his headmaster may even make it difficult for the latter to remember his name. A deputy head must be much more sensitive to the interpretations that a headmaster might put on any suspicion of a deviation from school policy or any suggestion of disloyalty to his idées fixes.

The elimination of the confidential reference and a forced reliance on testimonials would not only make for a greater accuracy in the latter but obviate the inordinate waste of time involved in making abortive applications. As a deputy head I often helped in the appointment of teachers by sorting out from a mass of applications those which were obviously unsuitable by reason of inappropriate qualifications. It was then that I discovered how insidious the occasional discrepancy between a testimonial and a confidential reference could be. A single phrase in the latter was sufficient to damn an application beyond hope of further consideration. I remember being outraged by a reference from a college tutor whose name had in all innocence and confidence been given by a young man seeking his first appointment. The character of this youth was so traduced in the confidences of his tutor as to destroy his chances of being appointed anywhere. I felt impelled to intervene. Fortunately I was able to get hold of his father's address and to pass on the advice that his son should disabuse himself of the idea that his tutor held him in any esteem whatever.

My own practice in writing references was to ask a teacher to brief me on all aspects of his work and career. It is surprising how in a big comprehensive it becomes impossible to be aware of all the activities of the staff. I always liked to be able to commend a teacher not only for considerations of which he was aware but for cheerfulness, a quality of great importance in a staff room during the last few weeks of term. My Headmaster rarely visited the three staff rooms and in this respect I was much better placed to comment on those qualities that make a man a good colleague. In some ways a deputy headmaster is in an invidious position. According to my contract with the Local Education Authority I was an 'assistant teacher'. As a member of the Assistant Masters Association I was subject to the professional code restraining me from commenting unfavourably to the Headmaster on any other assistant teacher. My place was in the staff room among my colleagues. This was all plain sailing in the limited size of a grammar school. It became very very difficult when, as deputy head of a staff which with all the part timers numbered a hundred, I was clearly expected to exchange confidences about my colleagues in my daily confabulations with the Headmaster. He was an active NUT man and as such was less inhibited by the convention of staff room confidentiality than I was. Even less aware of my sensitivity in this matter was the Assistant Director of Secondary Schools. When he visited the School for the purpose of investigating complaints from parents about the conduct of a teacher, he clearly had no qualms in asking me to comment on the case. I had to explain to him that although I was the Deputy Head I was also a member of the staff room and could not possibly discuss the failings of a colleague imputed to him by parents behind his back. The upshot was that I had my principles put to the test and had to pass judgements on the teacher in his presence.

Having said this much against the use of 'confidential' communications between headmasters in the making of appointments I have to concede that there must be some safeguard against the intrusion of charlatans and confidence men. This was brought home to the Headmaster and myself when we made an appointment in haste to fill a post which was still vacant after the beginning of term. Classes were in being which were not being taught. I received a phone call from a young man claiming to hold a degree in the appropriate subject. I made arrangements for him to come straight away and see the Headmaster. My suspicions about him were aroused soon after he began teaching. Among his pupils was my son, from whom I learned of the really remarkable diversity and distinction of the newcomer's accomplishments at the national and international level as an athlete and racing driver. This aroused my curiosity but not enough for me to question his credentials. His undoing was his attempt to sing. At a rehearsal of the chorus of a school production of a Gilbert and Sullivan opera we happened to be singing next to one another. His confident but unfamiliar rendering prompted me to ask him what part he was singing, whether tenor or bass. I was singing bass. He told me without hesitation that he was singing bass and resumed doing so with unembarrassed verve. My reaction was immediate. If he really believed what he said, and there was no doubt that he did, then he had a capacity for self-deception and fantasy that could embrace his claim to be a graduate of Cambridge University. Next morning I asked the Headmaster to check this point. The County Education Office made enquiries which revealed in the first place that he was capable of a carefree inconsistency in that he had gone on record to the County as being a graduate of London. It turned out that he was a graduate of nowhere. The County officials made more fuss about the matter, presumably because it involved gaining payments by fraud, than they would have been if he had had the right qualifications but been a hopeless teacher. Three officials came all the way across the county to settle the account before sending the miscreant on his way. The local tradesmen were dissuaded from prosecuting him for defaulting on substantial debts. His self-assurance seemed in no way diminished by his narrow escape from a criminal action. Not long afterwards he wrote asking for a reference and we heard that he had set up as an educational consultant.

The unfortunate and more permanent result of this affair was in the redoubled insistence of the County Education Office on resort to confidential reports on all applicants for teaching posts prior to selection for interview, a circumstance that slowed up the already tardy and inefficient procedure for filling staff vacancies.

The almost total exclusion of teachers from the crucial business of appointing teachers is part of a vicious circle the breaking of which there is as yet no sign. The majority of school governors and officials who are responsible for selecting teachers lack experience of teaching. The fact of this deficiency rarely if ever induces in them either humility or diffidence in the manner in which they discharge their task. On the contrary my discussions with appointing panels during my years as a deputy head left me with a firm impression of a patronising attitude among the sort of lay enthusiasts for education towards the teachers whom they were selecting to give effect to their often quite jejune ideas. At the same time it has to be admitted that the general level of sophistication, of education itself, among many of the young men now applying for teaching posts provides some justification for this condescension and for the implicit distrust of the ability of teachers to be regarded as a profession capable of controlling admission to its own ranks. To the political hacks among the governors, the certificated teacher was little more than a three-year-trained apprentice, while the graduate teacher needed to be watched for signs of bourgeois pretensions. To such governors the idea of pupil representation on governing bodies was much more acceptable than teacher representation. The educated governor – educated in the narrow sense of having gained a degree and reached a position of responsibility in a profession or in public service – could not fail to be influenced in his judgement of teachers by the obvious intellectual limitations of a significant minority of them. The only way to overturn this relationship between teachers and those who appoint them is to raise the calibre of entrants by a quite startling increase in salaries, something comparable to that gained by the miners in the last forty years. Unfortunately for teachers, consideration of educational objectives is a long-term business, and unlike power cuts and coal stocks, not noticeably a process easily or immediately affected by strikes.

I spent one term at the secondary modern school, its last as such before it became comprehensive. Most of this was spent in the company of the Headmaster observing what I could of the problems of running a school. I was lucky in being able to work my way slowly into my task of academic re-organisation, and it may surprise some that my first pre-occupation was not with the work of the School but with its appearance, with school uniform. That this was so was not in any way due to prejudice or preconceptions on my part. I flatter myself that I am a quick learner, and I learned very quickly from prospective parents that their preference for sending their children to the Grammar School was in large measure rooted in their distaste for the appearance of the secondary modern boys and girls. This was no surmise on my part. 'Look at them, just look at them!' There was no baulking this issue. It was as important to become a fully uniformed school as to enlarge the curriculum to include such subjects as Latin.

It took between two and three years to win unquestioning acceptance of uniform. In the first instance I worked at this problem almost single-handed, with the moral support of the Headmaster whose earlier attempts in this matter had provoked active opposition from the Trades Council. It was ironic that the socialist elements in the town proved to be, not only in this matter of uniform but also in the question of discipline and behaviour, the most purblind critics of our efforts to break down the most serious obstacle to becoming accepted as a credible alternative to the Grammar School, the image of a secondary modern school in the least complimentary use of the title. Soon, however, the Headmaster and the senior staff, particularly the ladies, supported me.

The only thing I ever learned from attending a weekend conference organised by the National Union of Teachers was the legal position of schools wishing to establish complete conformity of wearing a uniform. Strictly speaking it appeared that the wearing of uniform was not enforceable by sanctions. The Headmaster was within his rights in banning unsuitable items of wear such as studded leather belts. In practice it proved to be a problem amenable to persuasion. During the winter terms I always carried a pocketful of ties which I bestowed in as genial a manner as possible on boys, some of whom were wearing them for the first time. A stock of used blazers and other items were collected at nominal prices, sent to the cleaners and resold or given to the very small group of children whose clothing normally came from jumble sales. I visited homes and talked to parents whose antipathy to uniform stemmed from suspicion of schools. In the case of boys whose standing with their peers was based on an habitual disregard for the wishes of adults in general I made a point of asking them to accept a blazer or pullover as an example to others. Though at the time my preoccupation with school uniform must have seemed obsessive, in retrospect it appears as a successful exercise in persistence in the conduct of which I strove to avoid nagging, irascibility or censure.

The effect of becoming a fully uniformed school was quite remarkable. It surprised me. Not only did it dissipate much prejudiced hostility to the School, but it obscured the diverse social backgrounds of pupils. The small groups of leather-jacketed boys who assembled after school down the road became a thing of the past. Parents from nearby towns sought admission for their children. Occasionally a misguided egalitarian wrote a hostile letter to the local press – misguided because the school uniform proved an effective counter to social inequalities – but invariably was answered by letters from parents. Yet to my mind the greatest beneficiaries of school uniform were the pupils. Freedom in the matter of dress had been the means by which cultural affiliations were proclaimed. It is the mark of a truly professional teacher that concern is exercised impartially for all boys and girls alike. This is the ideal. In my view its attainment became a common feature of teaching practice in the School when a class of low-ability pupils was indistinguishable from those in the top band. This reflection is in no way invalidated by my lifelong sense of indebtedness to my own school where considerations such as I have adumbrated here did not obtain and where wearing uniform was voluntary.

The spectacle of a multitude of boys and girls converging on to the campus of a large comprehensive can be daunting and dispiriting. During the heyday of my decade as a deputy head this was not the case. I arrived at School at twenty minutes past eight. The boys and girls were supposed to be there between eight forty and eight fifty. In practice, however, so many mothers went to work on the industrial estate that the campus was alive with pupils as I stepped from my car. Sometimes my wife would drive me to work. According to her, my posture and demeanour on getting out of the car was that of a setter dog. I looked around, scanning the whole scene, the lawns that fronted Middle and Upper Schools on the north side of the road, and the playground and verges that lay between the Lower School and the south side of the road. For the new buildings that had been added as the School developed straddled a road which, by eight thirty, would be occupied by cars, bumper to bumper, on their way to the industrial estate.

This meant that there had to be rules governing the arrival and movement of over seventeen hundred pupils. These rules were particularly stringent for those who came by bicycle. All movement between the Upper and Middle Schools to the north of the road and Lower School to the south of the road had to be by the pedestrian crossing. This restriction applied to everyone, including myself, whatever the time of day while the School was in session, even after the rush hour traffic had disappeared and the road between the Schools had become almost deserted. I confess that the civilised aspect of this great influx, which was pleasing to those parents who observed it, was also a source of satisfaction to me. For it was a contrived achievement and one in which I was deeply involved. The lawns remained unscarred and the campus provided an attractive setting for all, including the pupils, to appreciate. The scene was one of ordered and relaxed movement, made all the more so by the scatter of royal blue uniforms which made the girls look deceptively engaging. Yet it was at this moment of surveillance, of maximum awareness and alertness with which I began each day, that I habitually reflected on the shortsightedness and ad hoc method of the school planners who were responsible for the palpable absurdity of the situations it was my business to control. I sometimes gave vent to my feelings to my wife: 'Madness, stark raving madness – bringing all these kids to the same place at the same time.'

CHAPTER III

THE MYTHOLOGY OF SECONDARY MODERN SCHOOLS

The Education Act of 1944 lays down the procedure which it is incumbent upon Governors and Local Education Authorities to follow when they decide to re-organise a secondary school. The relevant part of the Act is Section 13. According to the Act any re-organisation of a county secondary modern school, such as Hazelwick, laid on the Authority an obligation to allow an opportunity for objections by the posting of notices for a period of two months. In the case of Hazelwick the Authority, whose anxiety to push the matter through without arousing public interest seems in retrospect almost pathological, absolved themselves from this obligation by reference to the wording of Section 13 where it confirms the obligation to such changes as may be regarded as 'significant'.

I am still wondering just what it was that might have been regarded by my employers as a 'significant' change. Clearly my appointment as a Senior Academic Master charged with re-organising the curriculum and courses, not to mention the standards of a school, was a matter of little consequence. Yet my appointment, as well as those of the new Heads of English, Languages, Maths and Science, was accompanied by the assurance that the comprehensive character of the school was to be guaranteed by the inclusion in next year's intake of two classes of 'grammar school' pupils. Make no mistake about it. Without such an assurance none of us would have accepted the appointments. Yet the Governors and the Authority were not altogether unaware of the consequences of these two changes. A grammar school intake and a comprehensive school curriculum, if it was to amount to anything more than a window-dressing exercise, was going to increase the number of pupils remaining at school after the statutory leaving age of fifteen. Ultimately it was going to produce a sixth form of grammar school proportions, with all the attendant specialist accommodation and staffing.

In fact the decision to erect a completely new building to house the large Upper School which was to emerge had already been taken before my appointment. Indeed, my first major task as Senior Academic Master was to draft a curriculum for the whole school as it would be in 1967, the year in which the new comprehensive intake of 1960 would take A levels. Actually the impact of the teaching policies I established was such that the first A levels were taken by secondary modern pupils in 1964. However, I completed the draft for the 1967 curriculum in the last week of May 1960. At this point I want to be precise about what I have to say, not only because of my bewilderment at the official view that nothing of significance happened at Hazelwick, but also because of the subsequent change of attitude on the part of the Authority who, after the school had been well and truly established as a very successful comprehensive, placed upon us the additional responsibility of coping with as many as five hundred visitors a year.

On the 30th of May 1960 I accompanied the Headmaster to a meeting at County Hall where the Deputy Director and the local HM Inspector examined my draft curriculum. The object of the exercise was to calculate the size, area, and facilities to be included in the plan of the new building. The Inspector, a lady whose concern for the education of girls was probably more developed than mine, made a minor alteration to increase the provision for the teaching of Needlecraft. The Deputy Director was most impressive. With a rapidity of calculation that surprised me he translated my forecast of all the lessons in all subjects that would be taught to all classes and option groups in 1967 into a schedule of the requisite classrooms, laboratories and craftrooms. The number of square feet available for an assembly hall and dining area was also estimated, the whole total of floor space being finely and finally adjusted to the regulations laid down by the Ministry in respect of such matters. On the 27th of June the Governors were regaled with the details of these developments. Protocol did not allow me to be present at the meeting. Indeed, in view of the little notice accorded to the major role I found myself playing for the next twelve years, I am tempted to think that protocol precluded recognition of my existence as far as County Hall was concerned. However, the Headmaster was kind enough to tell me the day after the meeting that the Deputy Director had praised my draft curriculum to the Governors.

No significant change. In 1964 the new building for Upper School was opened. It consisted of six superbly equipped science labs, two for each of the natural sciences: Biology, Chemistry and Physics, together with prep rooms; there were three large classrooms, five sixth-form division rooms, a language laboratory, a Geography room, a splendid and spacious library, a new study for the Headmaster, a staff room, a sixth-form common room, and a combined assembly and dining hall. There was also accommodation for secretaries and the usual cloakroom provision. Such was the superiority of this new building in every respect over the two buildings that had comprised the secondary modern school that it almost became a mark of status for teachers to be based in Upper School, despite the fact that their teaching timetables might take them for considerable periods to lessons in Lower or Middle Schools.

While I suspect that the provision of a new building and the expenditure it involved might well have ranked high in the lists of the administrators' pre-occupations, there were other changes with which I was more closely and permanently concerned. Inevitably the school grew. The secondary modern Hazelwick had 952 pupils and a staff of 52. When it was fully developed as a comprehensive school, 1,760 pupils were taught by 104 teachers. This mere increase in size was not, I agree, in itself a matter of significance. More important in my estimation was the fact that in 1960 there was one class taking O levels at the end of a six-year course. There were no A level pupils or courses. During the years I was responsible for the work of the school the number of subject-passes rose from thirteen in 1964 to totals above a hundred. These results reflected not only a change in organisation and a new order of priorities but a gradual change in the composition of the staff. Above all the change in the reputation and standing of the school was nothing short of a revolution.

About three years after I became Senior Academic Master and Deputy Head I met the town Probation Officer at a party given by one of the Governors. 'What's happened at Hazelwick?' he said. 'We don't seem to see much of your pupils these days.' This was what I wanted to hear. It vindicated the bee in my bonnet. It matters not at all that you reclassify a secondary modern school as comprehensive. Nor does it signify a change of consequence if you include pupils of grammar school ability in the intake, or appoint more academically qualified teachers to teach them. Nothing important happens unless and until you teach them, and I mean all pupils irrespective of ability, as if their success meant as much to you as that of your own children. This was the real change for which I had to press, day in and day out, that all children should be given work which both matched and extended their abilities, that the interest taken by teachers in the work of their pupils should be as intense and sustained for those of low ability as for the 'high fliers'. If this sort of sentiment sounds suspiciously redolent of the pious platitudes to which one is treated on speech days I can only protest that seventy-five per cent of my own teaching time was with low-ability classes, despite the fact that I made my own timetable, and as a deputy head I was eventually free to give up teaching altogether. The tendency of teachers to treat lightly the endeavours of less able pupils is proved time without number by the choice of classes to assist in the occasional manual chores that crop up in all schools, such as arranging chairs for a concert, or assisting with the unloading of a lorry load of stationery. The syllabus of a low-ability form should be as immune from casual and fortuitous interruption as that of the top GCE class in the week before the exam. Fortunately my conviction that problems of behaviour are severely exacerbated by teachers who interrupt their lessons on what must appear to their pupils as trivial pretexts was shared by the Head of the Remedial Department, Mr G. Fryer, who came to Hazelwick in 1962. His concern that pupils in his Department should be shown the respect of being taught consistently invariably manifested itself when one of his teachers was absent. I would find him waiting for me, ready with plans for keeping the lessons going, even if he had to surrender all of his own preparation periods. It did not surprise me that his Department achieved remarkable results in raising reading ages of backward pupils, nor that their behaviour when abroad on continental school holidays won praise from observers.

It was on a fine summer evening in 1960 that the indifference of parents to what was afoot at Hazelwick was brought home to the Headmaster and myself. The Deputy Director and his Assistant for Secondary Schools arrived at the School to break the news to us about parental choices of school for the September intake. Of all those whose eleven-plus scores entitled them to choose between us and the other schools in the town, only four had opted to come to us. This information was imparted to us in a subdued and shamefaced way, as indeed it might well have been, in view of the promise of an uncreamed intake (made at the interviews in February) of two forms of grammar school pupils. Fortunately this was not the end of the matter. Towards the end of the term, the last of the secondary modern era, the list of names of our first comprehensive intake of eleven-year-olds arrived from County Hall. Close examination of eleven-plus scores revealed that the four volunteers had been augmented by a dozen children of borderline grammar school ability. The final position thus remained substantially unchanged. Hazelwick was to be launched as a comprehensive with minimal disturbance to the pecking order of the town's four secondary schools, with Hazelwick unambiguously at the bottom so far as public esteem was concerned. I was sobered by the magnitude of what had to be done to reverse this position. I was not used to working in schools of doubtful reputation. The LEA, on the other hand, could justify its proceedings by an absence of opposition reflecting the local indifference. The most galling feature of the situation was my discovery that parents, far from being re-assured by my having been sixth form master at the Grammar School, attributed my transfer to some sort of demotion.

Astrology is not a branch of knowledge that seriously engages my attention. Yet I was intrigued to learn from a reputable journal that my birth under the sign of Virgo accounted for qualities, which, according to my wife, I unmistakably possess: perfectionism, a critical attitude to myself and to others, a capacity for sustained hard work, and a desire for accuracy. If such is the case I suppose I can thank my lucky stars that I embarked on the task of nursing this very sickly baby of a school to strength and primacy with the advantage of having been born at the end of August.

In September I was joined by the four new Heads of Departments; they also evinced a predilection for hard work and precision of thinking, though whether they too had been born under Virgo I cannot say. In varying degrees they shared my chagrin at finding themselves in a severely 'creamed' school, and concern at the unevenness of the work expectations of the staff. The Head of Science, a PhD from industry, found that there was not a single science textbook in the School. His predecessor, who subsequently became a headmaster, did not believe in books. My own impression as I opened desks in all the classrooms and found them empty was that there was some sort of conspiracy to conceal from me what work, if any, was being done. Later I learned that it was the policy of the school to buy books in half sets and to gather them in at the end of lessons. More surprising was that a similar procedure applied to exercise books. As for the use of books for 'rough' notes, my enquiries were met with incomprehension. 'Writing is only allowed in best,' I was told.

What, in effect, I was discovering was a major element in the mythology of secondary modern schools, a legacy of the 1944 Act, a prevailing assumption that children who failed the eleven plus, with the exception of a favoured few who formed the top stream, were incapacitated by some innate tenderness of mind that precluded them from experiencing the stimulus of sustained concentrated academic work. It is to the incompetence of so many teacher training institutions that we must look for the source of this insidious belief. My grounds for this imputation derive from the number of my acquaintances who became lecturers in training colleges. None of those I have in mind had taught in secondary modern schools. This impression was re-inforced by the apparent anxiety of students who came from these institutions not to engage in any form of teaching that might involve incisive teaching on their part or sustained effort on the part of pupils. It is sometimes made a matter of reproach against grammar school teachers that some of them are 'untrained'. If this is so, let us be grateful. In my fifteen years as a grammar school master I learned to regard my work as a professional undertaking which it would have been an offence to disturb or interrupt. In fact I can only remember being called upon to leave a class once in all those years. What then, was I to think of one of my new colleagues whose class I came upon unattended and in uproar, and when I asked if there was some difficulty preventing the continuance of work, was told, 'It's all right; I am doing the Headmaster's flowers.' Another teacher, whose competence inspired respect, depressed my morale by asking that pupils taking part in the School play might be excused lessons for rehearsals. I made the obvious comment that this was an out-of-school activity. I was then told that as it was impossible to get pupils to remain at school after the end of lessons, the school play could only go forward by withdrawing children from lessons. It gives me satisfaction to record that within two years there were three or more major productions a year, involving large numbers of pupils, all of which were rehearsed after lessons.

Respect for truth, obligations of gratitude and a desire to put the record straight impel me to state that this problem of unevenness of standards was not so much a reflection of types of schools as of the date of training. Some of the secondary modern teachers, particularly the more senior, were a source of strength to the School. It would have been impossible if they had not been there. For this reason it gives me no pleasure to expatiate on the tensions which accompanied the task of establishing a high and common level of work standards. How I must have got on the nerves of these stalwarts with my comments at staff meetings about insufficient attention to marking and other aspects of teaching chores. There was, I suspect, an all-round testing of tolerance. My diary for the first year of the comprehensive school is punctuated with secret confessions of attacks of despondency. Fortunately I knew that I must never betray anything but an encouraging, cheerful optimism when at work. In one respect I was rewarded. There seemed to be nothing but relief that the days of changing policy with every new theory from the pundits were over. This relief was explicitly and gratefully expressed. The objectives had at last stabilised, and were safe from the lure of novelty and gimmickry. When I sat down in formal committee with the Heads of Departments to plan the routing of courses, examinations, reports and options, I insisted that we were planning and making decisions which, in their essentials, were not to be disturbed for at least ten years. One thing I had learned from past experience. Nothing saps the strength of a school more than a constant digging up of the foundations. Six years later I was able to refer to these decisions in writing my Academic Report to the Headmaster and the Governors as the basis of the success of the School.

There is an entry in my diary for the 10th of January 1961: 'A day of strenuous, incessant activity, interviewing, timetabling, consulting, advising, teaching, checking, planning, corresponding, promoting, admonishing, punishing, arranging and organising. Home to marking. Very tired.' I was not, of course, alone in immolating myself. The moments of sombre doubts were experienced by my immediate allies, the four new Heads of Departments. At one point when support from above seemed uncertain we seriously discussed whether it might not be more realistic to cut our losses and abandon ship. Over and above the problems of deficiencies of books and staffing there loomed what for us was the vital question of the intake. Was the Authority intending to fulfil the promise made to us at the time of our appointments of establishing an uncreamed comprehensive school? If so, how was this to be done without arousing implacable hostility from the parents concerned? With this weighty problem in mind we talked with the Headmaster, who shared our perturbation, and who was in any case the only channel of communication between us and the Authority.

When you come to consider the matter, teachers, with the exception of Heads, have a pathetically depressed status in their relations with those above them. The transformation of Hazelwick School, upon which the Governors and the Authority were so determined, depended completely upon the perseverance of the small group of teachers led by me for its success. Yet to this day I can only refer to rumour and gossip to account for the fact that our Headmaster's request that we should be allowed to confront the Governors was conceded. My diary records that at the Governors' Meeting in the autumn of 1960 the accusation was made that we, the new staff, were being defeatist, and that the Headmaster was able to make this the pretext of a meeting between us and the Governors on the afternoon of the 15th of November. Three things remain in my memory, as well as my diary, about this fateful meeting. I spoke first in terms which I intended to sound optimistic and which were aimed at refuting the charge of defeatism. At the same time I referred to what was for all of us the crux of the matter: the need for the Authority to fulfil its promise of a grammar school intake. The second feature of the encounter was the incisive aggressive attack on the total inadequacy of the Authority's provision for a successful re-organisation in every respect, made by the new Head of English. In his command of English, in his forceful personality and fearless character, Michael Tucker was a formidable protagonist. If men of his stature were less of a rarity among teachers, the authority of those set over them would be far less impregnable than it is. Finally I remember the contribution to the debate from the Deputy Director, a mixture of plausible explanation of the legal difficulties attending the direction of grammar school pupils to Hazelwick, and of pious exhortation to the effect that we had nothing to fear from the future if we did not lose confidence in ourselves. These well-intentioned sentiments revealed a misreading of the situation. If anyone had cause for worry it should have been the Deputy Director, for if he or the Authority were going to default on the matter of the intake, the experiment would have had to start again with new participants.

Just what legal technicality was devised to meet our demands I shall never know. All I know is that on the 28th of January 1961 the Headmaster arrived at school cock-a-hoop at the outcome of the Governors' Meeting held the previous evening. The children of our two neighbourhood junior schools were all, except only those with brothers or sisters at other schools, to come to us. Only one obstacle remained. Would the parents accept Hazelwick, a school still regarded by most of them as secondary modern of dubious reputation, or would they organise for the principle of parental choice.

The parents' reactions to these developments did not begin till March 1961. I received a confidential letter from the parents of a child at a junior school whose teachers had encouraged them in the view they should aim for a place at a secondary school which would ensure a place at university. I knew from experience that children who evince outstanding ability at eleven are not always the ones who leave school for Oxford or Cambridge. However I have every sympathy for parents who have nothing more on which to hang their hopes than the specious promises of Local Education Authorities. My own experience as a parent had taught me that the claims which accompany the opening of a new school do not merit more than the scepticism that is appropriate to a TV commercial. So I was careful to sympathise with their apprehensions and to confine my re-assurances to my well-justified confidence in the new Heads of Departments. Encouraged by my apparent detachment, the parents became bold enough to tell me what I had so long suspected, that there was almost universal antipathy of the parents of the most able pupils at the junior schools to Hazelwick. The reputation of the latter was low in respect of the behaviour of its pupils and the standard of their work. In my own view, based on my initial experience, their anxieties in respect of work standards were not unfounded. The problems of extra-mural unruliness, instances of which were cited by every dissident parent I met, were, I thought, partly due to their proximity to the School and in any case stemmed from the root problem of the limited demands made upon pupils in the classroom. The widespread respect which the School achieved in the next few years was significantly in step with the marked increase in the pressure of work imposed throughout the school.

This interview was merely the first of a number which occurred at intervals throughout the term. The total of parents involved was not large, but invariably the vehemence of their animosity to the re-organisation was expressed with an intensity that made us anxious that they should not coalesce and resort to a public meeting, or that the press should get wind of their grievances. These encounters therefore took place in their homes. My assurances about academic bona fides were supported by the presence of the Head of English and the Head of Languages, who agreed with me that the success of our persuasions would have little chance if some of the more vociferous critics of the School were afforded the chance of uncensored confrontation with the Headmaster. The meetings were clandestine. The press remained unaware of them, and missed the chance of blowing up this incipient protest movement to a size beyond our control. The one aspect, however, of this defusing operation which I still regret was that it enabled the Education Officers at County Hall to view the smoothness of the re-organisation with a satisfaction that took no account of the strenuous but unacknowledged advocacy we undertook on their behalf. The official version of the lack of resistance to the surrender of places at the Grammar School by parents living in the catchment area of Hazelwick remains to this day that no direction of pupils was involved. There was no violation of the principle of parental choice. How could there have been? It was illegal. The obvious and usual pretext for manipulations of this sort, an alleged shortage of places at the Grammar School, would not have stood up to examination, for, as the result of the success of our persuasions, the intake to the Grammar School had to be reduced that September by one form of entry. I should know. I earned the shouted reproach of one of the Grammar School staff for having 'pinched a stream', as he cycled past me on his way home from church. There was direction all right. The anger of the parents was not, as the Authority would have liked to believe, because they had the choice of an alternative to the Grammar School; they were angry because they had no choice.

When the list of entrants for September 1961 finally arrived it was clear that we had won uncreamed status. The climb from the bottom had become more than an outside possibility. Yet my feelings were mixed. I experienced the weight of inescapable obligation to succeed in order that the dubious means should be justified by the unqualified achievement of the end. Neither did it afford me any satisfaction that the policy and manner of proceeding of the County Education Officers precluded any recognition of the crucial nature of my part. Indeed, the pretence that nothing of significance had or was happening at Hazelwick was maintained with such success that the clerks at County Hall continued for the next two or three years to address all correspondence to the School not to Hazelwick Comprehensive School, but with the original secondary modern designation of 'County Secondary School'.

A few years later there was another re-organisation to complete a comprehensive system for the whole town. The Grammar School was combined with the secondary modern school that shared its campus. In theory the inclusion of an established grammar school should have made the re-organisation more acceptable than that based on a secondary modern school. This time, however, the Authority were not so lucky. There was no 'fall guy' to do the dirty work. The opposition from the Grammar School was organised and vociferous. There was no escaping public notices and the local press was not short of good copy.

The achievement of uncreamed status would obviously not make an immediate impact on the reputation of the School, though its effect on the morale of the staff was apparent from the beginning of the next academic year. Yet it was over two years later that controversy over the academic bona fides of Hazelwick appeared in the local press. The circumstances which gave it rise were trivial, if not bizarre, in comparison with the vehemence of our reaction. At an otherwise unremarkable public meeting to celebrate an occasion designated 'Education Week', one of those pointless, time-consuming affairs for which the National Union of Teachers never seems to lack funds, a large audience was honoured with an address from Sir Ronald Gould. At the conclusion of his impeccably uncontroversial speech a young parent rose to attack the zoning system introduced in 1961 and to deplore the disadvantageous effect on her child's chance of getting to university because the child would have to go to Hazelwick. Our investigation revealed that the infant in question was only three years old. Nevertheless, a columnist in the local paper who wrote under the pseudonym 'New Townsman' not only reported the incident but made it the subject of critical comment. I and the senior members of staff rejoined with long letters of assurance, giving details of our degrees, universities and previous experience in preparing entrants for universities. We need not have worried. Other letters appeared from Hazelwick parents, one of whom had been among the dissidents whom we had visited two years earlier, which said all that needed to be said to silence this belated attempt to stir dying prejudices.

This was in December 1963. Back in the summer of 1961 the climb from our position at the bottom of the local school league table was hardly begun. This was highlighted for us on a day when new staff were being interviewed. One of the applicants was a young man of exceptional candour. From him we learned what they thought of us at the much esteemed comprehensive on the other side of the town. He told us that when he attended an interview there, the soubriquet by which staff referred to Hazelwick was still 'the Dump'. This was, of course, less than a year since the School had been so furtively upgraded to comprehensive status. It is worth recording that in due time we reversed this situation to such an extent that the desire of parents to obtain places at Hazelwick included applications from all parts of the town. Meanwhile, during that first crucial year, we were almost hysterical in our efforts to obtain respectability. By 'we' I mean the Headmaster and the new senior staff. Indeed, one of my nagging doubts about our chances of success stemmed from my awareness of the apparent complacency of the old rank and file. Events proved me wrong. I underestimated the effect of precept and example.

The summer of 1961, despite the prospect of an uncreamed intake in the coming September, was marked by the climax of the tensions between the old and new order of things as meeting followed meeting to hammer out academic and administrative objectives, and the priorities and standards these involved. Internecine and mutual suspicions were quite fortuitously underlined by the fact that a meeting of Heads of Departments dealing with academic routine co-incided with an equally important meeting of Heads of Schools dealing with administrative and disciplinary organisation. These suspicions were in fact quite unfounded and stemmed from the ham-fisted way in which the re-organisation had been planned. On the other hand it was the abortive attempt of the County Councillor who, with the Deputy Director, had been responsible for the strategy adopted to make Hazelwick comprehensive, to intervene in our deliberations that largely resolved these perturbations. The panacea which he proposed was the adoption of a distribution of power and responsibility based on a division of the School into Houses. If there was any plan calculated to rouse all the senior staff to a united opposition and to create a détente between all factions, it was the prospect of a House system. I was not present at the meeting with the County Councillor. I was at home, laid low with lumbago and exhaustion. It was typical of the reaction which the prospect of this meeting engendered that my bedroom, far from being a refuge and a place of rest, was thrice visited for the purpose of agitated discussion by the Headmaster and the Head of English. When I returned to work I learned that the School had warded off the burden of a spurious administrative structure. It was both typical and gratifying that the Headmaster delegated to me the job of drafting our unanimous rejection of a House system in a letter to be signed in the last resort by the Chairman of Governors. House systems belong to boarding schools where their pastoral functions are based on the realities of full-time residence and the range of care it involves. The realities with which we had to cope stemmed from the physical division of the School into two, later three, separate buildings, the bases of Lower, Middle and Upper School pupils respectively. The pastoral and disciplinary problems of these three age groups differ to a degree about which I could expatiate at length. However, my responsibilities were primarily academic. The very successful pastoral organisation based on the three separate buildings was the creation of the Headmaster and the Heads of Schools.

The state of exhaustion to which this first year of comprehensive status reduced the Headmaster and his immediate assistants was, I am glad to say, never again quite so severe. It took its toll in the form of an end-of-term disagreement between the Headmaster and the Head of English whose impatience with the rate of change and inability to suffer fools among his colleagues with any pretence of gladness made him constantly critical. His resignation deprived me of a most vigorous colleague.

The trouble had arisen when Tucker, exasperated beyond bearing by what appeared to him as the inexcusable incompetence of the teachers appointed to administrative posts, felt the only remedy in a question that riled him more than most was to adopt the desperate device of a round robin petition to Keyte, as Headmaster. In the view of many of the staff, whom Tucker enlisted as signatories, the number of pupils being made prefects was so large that it had become a cause of embarrassment in the classrooms. Badly behaved and work-dodging pupils in the fifth year were, it seems, too often the ones chosen as prefects. Whatever the rights or wrongs of this particular allegation, the Headmaster reacted to what obviously appeared to him as an organised attack by new and more highly qualified staff on his own authority. His response to the round robin was one of immediate anger and aggressiveness. My first judgement of the situation was, however, kinder to him and less favourable to the formidable Tucker, whom I thought was rash to present the Headmaster with a typed quasi-manifesto couched in pungent terms. I subsequently became more used to the inflammable nature of the Headmaster's reaction when taken by surprise by criticism, especially when presented without any attempt at diplomacy or tact. What followed in this case left one in no doubt as to the need for these ingredients in all exchanges with the Headmaster.

After a lapse of a few days in which it might be thought that Keyte was giving dispassionate consideration to Tucker's document, Keyte sent for the wretched signatories, one by one, beginning with the least pugnacious and most inoffensive of his secondary modern teachers who, before the advent of the forceful Tucker, would never have dreamt of signing a request to discuss anything. Having reduced these miscreants to a proper sense of their own insignificance, the Headmaster embarked on the extraordinary procedure of interviewing the Heads of Departments singly, on separated occasions, with his two most trusted supporters, the Heads of Middle and Lower Schools, seated on either side of him as silent witnesses, lending the scene an almost comic similarity to one from a gangster film in which 'the boss' is given moral support from two of 'his boys'.

The Head of Maths was the first to be subjected to the indignity of this procedure. According to the Headmaster she was reduced to confusion and recanted her support for both the round robin and the criticism of the prefectorial system. Yet her own account of the interview was quite different. This discrepancy puzzled me. With experience I learned the need for interpretation of all such account of incidents, where the Headmaster's authority was involved. I came to understand what must be meant when it is said that a communication from a foreign state 'is being studied'. Be that as it may, the Headmaster seemed in no hurry to continue the interviews with the two remaining signatories who were new Heads of Departments, the Head of Modern Languages, a teacher of great reputation, a member of the Hispanic

Council and known to the publishers of language books, and Tucker himself, the Head of English. The former almost anticipated events by demanding to be seen by the Head and his bodyguard, such was her indignation at what she regarded as a want of professional courtesies. By this time, however, the Headmaster had become less belligerent, and his eventual discussion with these senior Heads of Departments bore no resemblance to the carpeting of members of his original staff.

The tensions of the first year of re-organisation were only temporarily abated by the settlement of the matter of the prefects. During the last few days of the Summer term, the last of the academic year, when all the staff were striving to complete reports, check their stock of books, attend meetings on the promotion of pupils, while at the same time keep a semblance of a teaching routine going, I noticed Tucker becoming ominously detached. His conversation was ceasing except for caustic strictures on the incompetence of the 'hierarchy' as the administrative teachers were called. I sensed a coming crisis.

On the last but one afternoon of the term the Headmaster was at last free to meet a committee we had set up earlier in the term to investigate possible ways of improving morale and discipline. Tucker was the Chairman of this committee, an attempt to bridge what was experienced as a gap between the rank and file of the staff and the Headmaster and his intimates. It produced a unanimous report, but although it included what seemed sensible suggestions, it inevitably also seemed to imply criticism of the Headmaster. I was not on the committee, nor did I attend the submission of its suggestions to the Headmaster. Indeed, the exercise might have been wholly successful if undertaken at the beginning of a term and had not taken on the character of another confrontation between two very strained and tired men, Keyte and Tucker, the former fearing the influence of the latter, and the latter impatient with what he regarded as the crass incompetence of the former.

The first I knew of the row that took place in the Headmaster's study was when Tucker burst into my room. 'He's chucked me out... the bloody fool. It's no good. He'll never learn.' It appeared that Keyte had suspended or threatened to suspend his Head of English, Mr Tucker. According to another Head of Department Tucker had tried to argue that the morale of staff was low and that this stemmed mainly from the fact that their best endeavours were rewarded only by criticism from above, that the Headmaster's only solution to deficiencies in the School was to blame his staff repeatedly. This onslaught predictably roused Keyte to accuse Tucker of scurrility. Tucker rejoined by accusing the Headmaster of being unwilling to listen to criticism, and of 'wasting our time in calling us together'. This exchange was ended by the virtual suspension of Tucker.

Although the two men met again the next day in an attempt to smooth over the difference, it was clear to me that either the School would soon lose an exceptionally energetic and outstanding Head of English or the tensions between the old and the new order would continue to sap our high endeavour. Against these fears I weighed the one solid achievement of the first year of the School's history as a comprehensive. We had secured an intake for September 1961, albeit by what some might regard as dubious direction, some thirty or so pupils who might otherwise have proceeded as a matter of course to the town's grammar school, in the neighbourhood of Ifield. It may mitigate the seriousness of this development, as far as the future of these children was concerned, to record that by the time they had reached the sixth form, the grammar school at Ifield had ceased to exist, except as part of another comprehensive. Mr Tucker left Hazelwick the next term and was not long in becoming a Headmaster of repute. The same was true of the Head of Lower School.

CHAPTER IV

AN UNCREAMED INTAKE: THE TEACHING OFFENSIVE

The impact in the second year of re-organising the new intake to include at least one class of eleven-year-olds for whom A levels could be a foregone conclusion, will be well understood by teachers concerned by the pre-occupation of parents with examination results. I doubt, however, whether parents who are not also teachers could appreciate how profoundly the success of the re-organisation was affected by this diversion of a comparatively small group of children from a grammar school to our comprehensive, or why the progress of these children should have been for those of us most deeply involved in the success of re-organisation a matter of such moment.

To most children and to many adults, teachers are not, in some indefinable sense, altogether human. The truth is that teachers in their innermost feelings about children are sometimes only too human: they are not always as good as they ought to be in concealing a very human preference for 'nice' tractable children as opposed to unpleasant and obstreperous children. Their reaction to minor infringement of rules can also be sometimes more emotional than effective. In so far as they do achieve and maintain a professional appearance of impartiality they deserve far more respect than they usually receive. For the truth about children is, as Bertrand Russell observed, that they are, like chocolates, very nice, until one is in a position to overindulge by working in a chocolate factory.

Now that juveniles are more and more obtruding upon the awareness of adults, notably as spectators at football matches, there is perhaps a growing sympathy for teachers who are confronted with the less agreeable aspects of juvenile behaviour every day at school; indeed, the tide is so far turning that one occasionally hears sympathy expressed for teachers, especially those who work in poorer urban areas. The best of these are those who are gifted enough to suppress or eliminate the frailty of their humanity and to maintain at all times a relaxed cheerfulness and competence whatever the odds.

If evidence were required that such teachers do exist in remarkable numbers, it consists in the sanguine confidence with which young people wish to emulate them, to undertake this most difficult of jobs. What induces them to do so is the vision of themselves in charge of a class of attractive and responsive children, to whom they will appear as a benevolent and omniscient source of interest and knowledge. I was in fact once told by a sixth former, in the course of an informal bus-stop conversation, how agreeable it must be to play this role. So strong is this image among many student teachers that even the most harrowing of their experiences during teaching practice does little to dispel the felicitous vision of the satisfactions to come. What makes a teacher continue to teach is quite a different matter, consisting chiefly of the difficulty of getting out of it. Inertia and habit also weaken the will. Statistical survey has revealed a low job satisfaction among teachers combined with a high degree of job stability. Like marriage, teaching can be entered upon with comparative ease and enthusiasm. It is not so easy to disengage.

To nourish expectations which a close and detached consideration of realities would soon dissipate is a sign of human frailty. It is a human failing to imagine children as collectively attractive, as collectively tractable, and, above all, as gratefully responsive to the good will and concern that you entertain towards them. It is also an illusion to imagine that, as in the case of some graduates, an enthusiasm for a subject in which one has excelled can be easily communicated to all and sundry. I defy anyone to interest me in the workings of the internal combustion engine. Even when my friends are trying to explain the reason for some defect in my own car I have to struggle with an immediate and total cessation of attention on my part.

The point of these reflections on the transience and elusiveness of the glamorous aspect of teaching is to throw light on what amounts to a confession. I do not think that I overstate the case when I say that the arrival of the 'grammar school' intake at Hazelwick provided for us an experience in teaching in which reality most nearly corresponded with fantasy. I speak, of course, for myself. I find it difficult to believe I do not also speak for my colleagues, those who shared in the teaching of those delightful and tractable eleven-year-olds. These were the bright ones whose eagerness to learn was the basis of our hopes to establish and vindicate the academic reputation of the School. Do not misunderstand me: I have always thought of myself as a professional, and would have condemned myself if I had betrayed a preference for particular pupils or classes. If I appeared irascible, it was because I deemed it the appropriate response to a particular situation. It has to be admitted that it would be difficult to sustain such a claim for the teaching body as a whole. A teacher who inveighs against a child and calls him or her 'stupid' would not be impossible to find. Yet the resort to such terms is as useless and as unprofessional as the standing of a doctor who abused a patient for being ill. Similarly it is for most teachers a more agreeable stint to teach children whose parents have already done half the job for them, in so far as the children possess a reasonable command of English and the restraints of good manners. Yet any assumption that these acquired advantages were a final proof of merit and value to the community would be not only unprofessional but a naïve lack of awareness of the realities of the adult world. Our society abounds in well-spoken villains, and self interest may be pursued with more subtlety by the erudite.

Having said this much, it can be a matter of candid confession that at that particular juncture, September 1961, and having regard to the vicissitudes that preceded their arrival, we regarded these children with a relish which, in any other context, would have been unwholesome. We liked them. By 'we' I mean the small group of Heads of Department who saw their immediate role as the founders of an academically successful school. I am sure that none of our first 'grammar' intake, the 1961 intake, as we continued to call them, had any inkling of the significance we attached to their future success, or the effect of their arrival on the morale of Heads of Departments. The matter is better understood by those who know that there are comprehensives and comprehensives, the great division between them being the extent to which they are creamed or uncreamed by a neighbouring grammar school. From then onwards I was able to state unambiguously in all descriptions of the School that were sent to university appointments boards, for circulation among their graduates in training as teachers, that 'no other school with grammar school provision serves the pupils of this catchment area.'

The previous academic year had ended with uncertainties and internal tensions that threw doubt on the future development of the School. The second academic year following re-organisation, however, was not far advanced before one sensed that the re-organisation and all the changes it implied had come to stay. The impact of the new order was at first more evident in some parts of the School than others. It is now more generally realised by those whose business it is to sponsor the re-organisation of schools that there is much more chance of success if new developments are built on new intakes at the stage of transfer from junior schools. This was a lesson we did not need to be taught. The fourth year classes contained many boys and girls whose attitude to school had already hardened to an intention to leave school as soon as possible. The hard core was a representative group, to be found in varying strength in all non-selective schools. Their intransigence became more easily understood if and when one met their parents. Any hostility to schools as such precluded the minimal degree of sophistication to enable them to distinguish one type of school from another. This indifference to anything that did not affect their immediate situation effectively insulated them from any understanding of our purposes or pre-occupations. There was little to be done but to allow them to complete their schooling on the terms to which they had become conditioned. It was surprising how soon this intractable element disappeared from the scene.

The immediate beneficiaries of re-organisation were undoubtedly the top-ability classes of the former secondary modern school. In what might be regarded in retrospect as a moment of indiscretion, the Deputy Head whom I was to succeed remarked to me that a target of three, or at most four, O levels seemed appropriate to the GCE fifth formers of the secondary modern intake. We did not discuss the matter. The new Heads of Department proceeded, as they would have done in any school, to increase the pressure of work. In this they were followed by newly appointed staff and the more perceptive of the original staff. It was a curious fact, however, that the most persistent and demanding of the new teachers was perhaps the Head of Science, Dr Llewellyn, who came to the School not from a grammar school but from industry. It was mainly as a result of his enthusiasm that four secondary modern boys who had been coasting along, taking six years to achieve their ration of O levels, were able to start on an A level course in Physics and Maths two years after re-organisation, three years ahead of the schedule for the emergence of a sixth form. I also took a hand in this teaching of secondary modern GCE classes. In taking a third year class of pupils who had entered the School two years before it became comprehensive, I discovered a boy, presumably an eleven-plus failure, whose quickness of response and understanding was such that I made a mental note that here was a potential Oxford or Cambridge entrant. I said nothing to this effect at the time. Experience has taught me to refrain from long-term forecasts. In due course, however, we met again for lessons when he reached the sixth form. He gained his place at Oxford, the first to do so as a result of the new order of things. The first secondary modern boy to gain a university place had in fact done so two years earlier. Subsequently he was awarded a postgraduate position at London University. He was a beneficiary both of Dr Llewellyn's drive and my flair for talent spotting, for I had reduced his O level course by a year soon after I met him in class. It is rarely, if ever, that my swans turn out to be geese.

The appointment of Mr C. W. Baker as Head of Lower School in 1962 was a great boost to the policy of giving primacy to academic standards. The usual tendency among Governors and County Officials is to discount academic qualifications and antecedents in filling administrative positions. This is a mischievous failing. Administrators deal with problems demanding immediate attention. The end product of teaching, on the other hand, may not be assessed until as long as five years later. The temptation to interrupt and rob the timetable of lessons is a major weakness of the large comprehensives with their pretentious administrative hierarchies. Mr Baker's support in achieving an impeccable standard of administration and discipline in Lower School, while maintaining an avid interest in teaching standards, diminished the area of this conflict for the ten years which ended with his departure for a headship.

In 1963 I was able to relinquish the Headship of Upper School when a permanent appointment was made. This was not only a lightening of my load but also a bonus for the Headmaster. The building of Upper School was well under way. The Headmaster had good grounds for complaint at my reluctance to be diverted from academic pre-occupations to a detailed consideration of purchases of equipment and furniture. The choice of Mr D. Wright as Head of Upper School did much to mitigate the severity of my opinions of Governors. He applied himself to the business of furniture with shrewdness and zest. Yet, like his colleague across the road in Lower School, he remained a man of grammar school priorities. Teaching was our business. Under Don Wright the Upper School and the growing sixth form got off to a good start, with the administrative function serving the teaching timetable, not eroding it. Like Bill Baker, Don Wright left for a headship. His successor as Head of Upper School, Norman Morland, continued the tradition and in his turn departed for a headship. I often wonder whether the departure of these three Heads of Schools together with that of some very able Heads of Departments was a factor in hastening my own retirement.

The 1961 intake was the first 'uncreamed' intake. Yet its exceptional character did not derive from this fact alone. Indeed, there were subsequent intakes which, in terms of the questionable yardstick of eleven plus, included a larger number of children with high Intelligence Quotients. The reluctant entrants of September 1961 did more than any other intake to establish the reputation of the School. This was not fortuitous. It proves a point. The determination of those of us to justify our demand for an uncreamed share of the 'grammar school' intake of the town as a whole meant that nothing in the teaching of these children was to be left to chance. The interest of the new Heads of Department and myself for the next five years was unrelenting. Before that time had elapsed three of the Heads of Department appointed in 1960 had gone. Dr Llewellyn died suddenly in his prime. The Head of English and the Head of Maths had moved on to better positions. The Head of Modern Languages alone remained of the original team. Indeed, she remained until her retirement which took place after my own resignation. She is thus in a sense my chief witness. I was in the key position for ensuring that nothing in the timetable or administration should weaken the teaching offensive. And what was proved was the foreseeable and the obvious; the deployment of the maximum teaching ability, with consistency and intensity, on a selected class of top ability produces optimum results. 'Nil bonum nisi optimum,' as they say.

This formula was never again, in my time, made the basis of staff deployment. The next year I felt confident enough to timetable in a truly comprehensive style. The best teachers were allocated at all levels. A greater share of the GCE work was passed to less experienced teachers. The readiness to teach less able children became a sine qua non of appointments. The fruit of this policy was a steadily increasing exam entry with steadily improving results. Yet the character achieved by the 1961 intake remained unique. I am not good at remembering names. Of the thousands of the boys and girls I have taught, I can recall the names of but a few. Yet the names as well as the faces of that select group, whose success had to be a gilt-edged security, are still with me. I do not labour the point because I have not fully made it until I add that, although we set out to fulfil a purely academic obligation to parents who had hoped for places at the Grammar School, our success was exceptional in all other respects. It seems that first-rate teaching by first-rate teachers ensures a great deal more than exam passes.

What started as a purely academic assemblage of eleven-year-olds developed into a social group with an unusual degree of cohesion. This social cohesiveness was not that of a mere like-minded clique, but provided the context for the stimulus of developing and lively minds, each upon each. It became most apparent after they had left school, in the extent to which they kept in touch despite geographical dispersal. The sixth form which emerged from our sustained concern contained more outstanding personalities, both boys and girls, than any other comparable group in any of the schools in which I have taught. For the sake of truth and accuracy I must qualify this panegyric. There was one notable dropout, a tough resilient character with an exceptional capacity for avoiding work, a capacity which he evinced from the day he entered the School, and which reflected, as is so often the case with the cheerful work-dodgers, a parental rejection of schooling. When all the usual pedagogic pressures proved unavailing I received the inevitable suggestions for a demotion. Let me stress that it was a matter of policy with me which was maintained consistently, except when over-ruled by the Headmaster, that no boy or girl should be demoted to a class or stream for academic failure which stemmed from laziness. The mischief that a disaffected intelligent pupil can cause when dropped into a group of their intellectual inferiors had been immediately apparent to me when I had found it in practice on my arrival at the secondary modern school. The Head of the Remedial Department was rightly incensed at any attempt to use his classes as a place for the relegation of the resolutely work shy.

One of the reasons for the exceptional activity of the 1961 pupils in out-of-school activities was the time devoted to Music. High standards were sustained by this comparatively small group of school musicians. The new Head of Music, Mr R. Keates, had an enthusiasm and ambition which extended the sweep of the new broom. A pattern of concerts, choral and instrumental, of carol services, and of musical productions was built up as the 1961 pupils progressed through the School. In 1966, in the term before O levels, their performance of The Mikado gave exceptional pleasure. In my view, however, the apogee of these activities was in their dramatic productions. I have seen many school plays, but Mr Weeks-Pearson's production of A Midsummer Night's Dream in 1968 was enthralling, an experience neither to be expected nor vouchsafed, in the world of amateur dramatics, more than once in a lifetime. Which is another way of saying that in Mr Weeks-Pearson these pupils had contact with a man of genius.

In the Autumn term of 1966, the term in which the 1961 pupils entered the sixth form, there was a significant addition to extra-curricular activities. The Staff and parents were invited to an entertainment, a Sixth Form Review. I think most of us went reluctantly in the expectation of the tedium of a jejune production. How wrong we were. The feast of riotous mirth to which these pupils treated us took us completely by surprise. No one, from the Headmaster downwards, myself included, was exempted from the satire and caricature which had been written with the lightheartedness of a jeu d'esprit. Let it be noted that Hazelwick was a school run on traditional lines, 'square' rather than 'with it'. When these youngsters portrayed the much cherished institutions of school life - Speech Days, School Assemblies, the mysteries of UCCA, the pretensions of the Advisory Youth Service – the sophistication of their perception was devoid of animosity or any trace of alienation. For me it was more than an evening of hilarious entertainment. It was proof of the total success of an enterprise, the vindication of perseverance by determined teachers whose only spur was an uncompromising belief in exacting but self-imposed standards.

I do not think that those educationists who propagate 'liberal' ideas of what a school should be would have been pleased with our success. These pupils not only wore school uniform, the same for sixth formers as first formers, but they showed no sign of wanting to do otherwise. When the Headmaster initiated a discussion of possible changes in the attire for sixth formers it fizzled out in the boredom it evoked. Another occasion when their conformity in the matter of uniform was most apparent was when they took part in a joint discussion with the sixth form of a comprehensive on the other side of town. It seemed to me that more relaxed discipline of the latter had induced a petulance and querulousness in debate that contrasted very unfavourably with the composure and dignity of our sixth formers.

In the last week of the Summer term of 1968 we were treated to another entertainment from the musicians of what had now become the upper sixth. It was staged as a farewell concert; an informal affair, but a celebration of a shared seven-year experience. The programme reflected versatility: a jazz band, an orchestral ensemble, solos composed by the more talented performers, American-style barber-shop singing, and a choral version of school rules. I sometimes wish that I could have afforded to have made my exit as a teacher at the same time as these lads and lasses. Physically I was in need of a rest. Psychologically it would have been the right moment. In 1960 I had undertaken to give a minimum of five years to the job, but it would have taken a smarter man than me to find as rewarding a post, in both senses of the term, at the age of fifty plus. I stayed for another five years but things were never quite so good again.

This eulogy of a comparatively small group of pupils leaves me wide open to criticism. I hasten to rebut it. The eight years following re-organisation were marked by changes in the work and achievements of the whole school. Furthermore both O level and CSE results continued to rise after the departure of the 1961 intake. I intend to recount these endeavours and to indicate that our concern embraced the problems of all our pupils. The fact, however, which is most pertinent to this part of my narrative is that we had insisted that no secondary modern, least of all the one in which we had become involved, could compete with a grammar school or could achieve comparable standards and enjoy equal esteem unless it included a fair proportion of grammar school pupils in its intake. In fighting on this issue we had, as it were, put our money on our own abilities to prove the point. Our intransigence in our argument with the Authority was matched by our intransigence as teachers. 'What is it like, being the top school?' I was asked by my good friend the Vicar, a man capable of viewing all these developments with detachment. We had proved our case.

CHAPTER V

THE CHARADE
WAS EXHAUSTING ...

Hazelwick School was not the first comprehensive to be established by West Sussex. The Thomas Bennett School had been opened in circumstances which augured well for its success two years earlier. Since it was launched with the advantages of new buildings, and a completely new and highly qualified staff, there was no danger of parental opposition. On the contrary the admission of the first intake was preceded by a highly successful public relations exercise, the effect of which lasted for many years. The whole operation was thus the antithesis of the re-organisation of Hazelwick secondary modern, in which the desire to minimise public interest involved the Authority in a procedure, a denial that anything really significant was happening, that bordered on chicanery. There was, of course, nothing illegal about my appointment as Senior Academic Master or my subsequent promotion to Deputy Head in 1962. Its significance lay in the fact that it relieved the Authority and the Governors of the embarrassment of having to assess publicly the suitability of the Headmaster and the Deputy Headmaster to run a comprehensive school assisted by a predominantly secondary modern staff. I have no intention of giving my own verdict on this matter. The fact that I was appointed suffices to underline the reluctance of the Authority to put the issue to the test of public opinion, of an open declaration of intent to re-organise, either with the Headmaster and his Deputy solely responsible for a new academic organisation, or the appointment of a new Headmaster whose qualifications were such as to secure parents' support.

As it was, my appointment as Senior Academic Master was a stratagem that amounted to a gamble on the ability of two men, one a very secondary modern headmaster, the other a very grammar school sixth form master, to learn to work a commonly agreed policy, towards common objectives and standards. There has never been a hint that anyone from the Director downwards ever had the least inkling of how much they were asking of both of us. It ought not to have worked. The self-abnegation demanded of both of us was way beyond the limits of the reasonable. I cannot respect either the intelligence or the integrity of those who imposed the psychological stresses for which they were responsible and of which they maintained an invincible ignorance.

As Senior Academic Master I was allocated the position of number three in the staff hierarchy. When I say 'number three', I mean it both literally and metaphorically. It was, of course, necessary for administrative purposes, particularly the timetable, to use some sort of shorthand code with which to refer to members of staff. Timetabling would have been impossible, having regard to the time available and the size of staff, if numbers had not been substituted for names of teachers. The trouble was that the numbers were allocated in such a way as to indicate the status of teachers precisely, as the results of school examination are used to place pupils in some schools, though not, I am glad to say, at Hazelwick. If the purpose of this numbering of staff was not intended to establish a refined gradation of status, then I can only aver that this was its unequivocal effect. I was told by rank and file members of staff of the intensity of feeling with which they examined the numbered order of the staff nominal roll at the beginning of each academic year, to discover whether they had gone up or down in the world. When, as a result of the promotion of the Deputy Head to a headship, I moved into his post my first act was to remove this pernicious administrative device and to replace it by an alphabetical nominal roll. My own number moved, with the changes and increase in staff from thirty to sixty.

My appointment as Deputy Head was made in a manner that indicated to me all too clearly how easily the Authority, the men at Chichester, forgot the crucial nature of my appointment as Senior Academic Master and its importance in getting the re-organisation accepted and functioning. In my first year at Hazelwick I was repeatedly assured that, in the event of the departure of the Deputy Head, my post as Senior Academic Master would automatically be combined with the Deputy Headship, to which I should succeed. Mr Henry, the County Assistant Director for Secondary Schools, went so far as to refer to my future in the encouraging terms, 'when you are a headmaster…' The Headmaster himself offered a wager that I would earn a headship within three years.

On the other hand I was apprised of sinister snippets of gossip which should have served to warn me against attaching much significance to assurances from anyone. Following a Governors' Meeting at which Mr Parker, the Deputy Director, had represented the Authority, it was reported to me by the Headmaster that the former had expressed his doubts as to my suitability for the post of Deputy Head because of 'my fondness for the cane'. Not only was I incensed by this unfounded calumny, I was from that moment made aware of the remoteness of County officials and their ignorance of the situations they attempted to manipulate. The exercise book in which I recorded all details of corporal punishment was never inspected. After Parker's inept comment I kept it in more than necessary detail. Another illusion which I shed at this time was the belief, instilled in me at the time of my going to Hazelwick, that I was to enjoy the support of those who prompted me to apply for such a difficult assignment. The most charitable explanation of the cessation of all communication, guidance or advice between myself and those responsible for dropping me, like an intelligence agent, into enemy territory, was that they suddenly recollected that the School still had a headmaster. The minimal interpretation of my ad hoc role was that I was appointed to advise him. It does not seem to have occurred to anyone how my ambiguous status could have in any way affected the re-organisation at all if he had exercised his undoubted right to ignore or override me. Fortunately, and again the Authority can consider themselves lucky, he welcomed me as a deus ex machina to a degree that at times I found embarrassing. On the other hand there were days when the contrast between his accustomed ways and my recommendations caused him to over-react into an assertion of his legitimate authority. For example, I took the view that the immensity of the task of raising of academic standards made it imperative that every consideration should be given to advice and requests from the senior Heads of Departments. In terms of status and graded posts they were the equals to their administrative opposite numbers, the Heads of Middle and Lower Schools. In my temporary capacity as acting Head of Upper School I was in both camps. It did not come easily to the Headmaster to break a habit of many years, the daily consultation with his familiar administrators, at which the Heads of Departments upon whom so much depended were liable to be discussed like any junior member of staff.

It took me about a year to get the hang of the situation. I was to pull the chestnuts out of the fire, but I was to expect no recognition or advice. For the lack of the latter I remain very grateful. Subsequent re-organisations, particularly that of the two schools, grammar and secondary modern, comprising the Ifield campus, revealed how lucky we were to be left alone to evolve as a comprehensive school in our own way. On the other hand if someone with power to influence events had deigned to spare half an hour to discuss some of the problems I encountered, no harm and much good might have been done. There was one exception to this absolute adherence to the rule that no consultation is permissible with anyone except the Headmaster. In 1966, by which time Hazelwick had risen to primacy among the comprehensive schools, it was decided by West Sussex that a conference of Heads and Deputy Heads should be held to discuss problems of re-organisation for the benefit of those schools for whom this fate lay in the future. I was pressed by Mr Parker, the Deputy Director, to speak at this conference. I did so with a certain degree of reluctance. The audience would consist both of grammar school heads and those from secondary moderns. How was I to speak with uninhibited candour on what I had discovered to be the most intractable of all problems: the creation of schools with organisations and standards in which both could give of their best without the inevitable tensions of suspicion and misunderstanding? Be that as it may, I said my piece without concealing my convictions that success depended on the uncompromising adoption of grammar school standards. I adduced evidence of the benefits of such a policy permeating the whole school. My speech was diplomatic in that I made my views clear without mentioning the two types of schools, but rather by a reasoned repudiation of the Newsom Report. In fact I stated without reservation that a good comprehensive was one that contrived, as we had done at Hazelwick, to whittle away the supposedly ineducable 'Half our Future'. In his introductory remarks to my speech the Deputy Director went so far as to refer to me as the one man in the county who was most qualified to talk on the difficulties of re-organisation and how to solve them. This was praise indeed. It re-inforces my conviction that this was a sentiment, sincere or insincere, which it was permissible to utter in the context of a conference of assembled head teachers but which would have involved a breach of protocol if said in the confines of my Headmaster's School.

When, in the Easter term of 1962, Mr Round resigned the deputy headship of Hazelwick, I reminded the Headmaster of the assurances I had been given, in informal manner, that I should automatically succeed Round. With understandable embarrassment the Headmaster informed me that it would depend on the view of the Assistant Director for Secondary Schools, Mr Fisher. In due course Mr Fisher arrived from Chichester and subjected me to a cursory interview. Once again my ingenuous trust in public servants, particularly those like the Deputy Director and his Assistant for Secondary Schools who had benefited from the formative and civilising experience of an Oxford education, proved misplaced. The informal assurances that my post as Senior Academic Master would be combined with those of Deputy Head proved worthless, and I was completely mistaken in my belief that the scope and success of my endeavours in making the re-organisation acceptable had earned me automatic promotion. I was surprised when the County decided to advertise the Deputy Headship, not as a mere formality, but as the prelude to fully competitive interviews. The worthlessness of encouraging and appreciative utterances, unbacked by legally binding communications, was thus brought home to me rather late in life. I have since made some use of the experience by stressing the need for scepticism about promises from public servants to my son, who is working for a government department. My disappointment was re-inforced by my incredulity that West Sussex could afford to set a precedent of appointing another Deputy Head while still retaining me as Senior Academic Master, instead of taking the chance of abolishing the anomaly of the two posts in one school. Indeed, when it became clear to me that they could consider appointing someone other than myself to replace Mr Round as Deputy Head, I reconsidered my position very seriously. If I refused to apply for his post I could enjoy a continued control of the work of the School but minimise my responsibilities. The prospect of less frequent conferences in the Headmaster's study was very attractive. The County, on the other hand, seemed to me to be laying itself open to a significant increase in staffing costs if future re-organisation involved acceptance of the pattern they were in danger of following at Hazelwick. The incalculable factor upon which my meditations centred was the possibility of the appointment of a new Deputy Head who might prove to be as self-effacing, albeit as conscientious, as Round had been, in which case I could only look forward to a re-inforcement of all tendencies to regression to a secondary modern school. Regression to the past is a natural reaction in all of us when we are subject to unusual stress or tension. Such moments were still frequent at Hazelwick and their effect was to make me think and feel as a grammar school teacher, and my headmaster as a secondary modern one.

After a period of agonising indecision I formally applied for the post of Deputy Head. I had, however, resolved that if a strong candidate appeared at the interviews I would withdraw in his or her favour. The short list consisted of eight or nine applicants selected from a large field. The Governors were present in force and the County was represented by the Assistant Director for Secondary Schools. Interviewing began in the morning with the preliminary scrutiny by the Assistant Director and the Headmaster. The interviews with the Governors were long and did not finish until eight o'clock in the evening. During the interminable waiting to be seen, the applicants were confined together in a small study in Middle School. This gave me ample opportunity to assess each and all of them. In the more relaxed and informal discussions that took place next day, when all was settled, it was generally agreed that the selection for the short list had fortuitously assembled a group of applicants, who, whatever their paper qualifications may have indicated to the contrary, proved at interview to evince a remarkably common appearance of mediocrity. There was, however, one candidate who gave the impression of being the exception to this depressing judgement. I decided to withdraw if I gained the least intimation that his outstanding superiority was revealed in his interview. Unfortunately the man must have known his own worth, for he decided to withdraw his application immediately after the preliminary encounter and did not wait to meet the Governors. I was left with a conviction, which became more and more firm as the time spent with the remaining candidates grew longer, that it was imperative for me to be appointed Deputy Headmaster.

My interview with the Governors was not altogether a happy one. In my talks with the Headmaster during the previous week I had been at pains to stress that if my post as Academic Master was to be combined with that of Deputy Headmaster, it was both essential to the efficient running of the School and a proper consideration of the load of responsibility I would carry, that the appointment of a permanent

Head of Upper School should be undertaken as soon as possible. Once more I was given assurances that subsequently proved worthless. At the conclusion of the cross-examination by the Governors, I was offered the post of Deputy Head. I attempted to make my acceptance conditional on an undertaking that I should be relieved of the role of Head of Upper School when I became Deputy Head. The Rector of Crawley, who was, if my memory is not at fault, the Chairman, treated my stipulation with scant seriousness and little patience. Clearly the day had gone on long enough without its prolongation by the consideration of such side issues. When I referred to assurances that such an appointment would be made, the Headmaster failed to remember that any such had been given. Thus it was that for one term at least the West Sussex Education Committee gained bargain value for the salary they paid me, a Deputy Head who was also Head of Upper School and Head of the History Department. When at the end of the Summer term of 1962 I encountered Her Majesty's Inspector on a visit to the School my fatigue was not to be concealed. There were inexplicable though fortunately painless streaks across my eyeballs. I reflected ruefully that we teachers offer little trouble to our employers, in marked contrast, for example, to the highly organised school-caretakers of the town, who were led by the Secretary of the local Trades Council, and who monitored any change in well-defined stints of work with a firmness not to be so casually brushed aside as was my own incipient attempt at bargaining.

On the other I should be guilty of hypocrisy if I did not confess that the same meeting of Governors defined my role in such terms as made me in effect perhaps the most powerful Deputy Head in the land. Indeed, the most important contribution to the discussion which preceded the formal offer of the Deputy Headship to me was made by Councillor Robert May. He insisted that whatever the scope of my responsibilities as Deputy Head, I was to retain the exclusive responsibility for academic organisation.

To do justice to the Headmaster I enjoyed complete freedom of action for the next five years in such matters as curricular schemes, the arrangement and sequence of examinations, the introduction of a Report Book for pupils, the transfer of pupils within the School and such purely academic matters as option schemes and their mediation to pupils and parents. In addition I took over the all-important burden of making the timetable. I suspect that a more typical

Headmaster than Mr Keyte would have taken the opportunity to develop a more reflective and supervisory role, and availed himself of the opportunity to move informally among his staff. This, however, would have involved a distortion of the Headmaster's nature far beyond reason. He remained pre-eminently a man of action and of little reflection. His study remained the bridge of the ship, whence came with unfeeling frequency the summons to his most senior staff to meetings of utmost urgency. Storms had to be weathered and, as any teacher who served at Hazelwick can testify, if crises did not occur in the course of events, then a crisis would soon be proclaimed on some pretext which justified a gathering of the wretched and harassed Heads of schools, at ten minutes' notice, unusually at break, in the Headmaster's study.

My term of office as Deputy Headmaster thus began in April 1962. It terminated with my resignation in April 1972. To the layman the success of a school, its reputation and standing, are identical with those of its Headmaster. Yet the role of Senior Academic Master had already conferred on me responsibilities normally undertaken by the Headmaster. In making me Deputy Head and in specifically reserving to me these well-defined responsibilities, the Governors, guided by the Deputy Director, Mr Parker, were making me Deputy Head Extra-ordinary. They were in effect making a school run by a diarchy. In so doing they were placing both the Headmaster and myself in an intolerable position, the root of which lay back in their lack of moral courage when, in 1959, they shirked the choice of decision to retain, with his powers intact, or to displace as unsuitable, the Headmaster of the existing school. It was soon made very clear to me that the Education Officers at Chichester wanted to have their cake and eat it. Protocol was sacrosanct. In all the ten years of my Deputy Headship they never failed to accord to the Headmaster all the considerations rightly due to his office and the weight of his responsibilities. I was no more regarded or consulted than the most junior member of staff. Yet I jealously regarded my role as being precisely defined at my appointment. The Governors and the Officers at County Hall changed as the years passed. Crawley became an 'excepted District' with its own Education Officer. Even the residents, who formerly shook their heads in dismay over the state of affairs at the School in its secondary modern days, forgot. The reputation of the School as a comprehensive became widely acknowledged, and with it the reputation of its Headmaster.

Meanwhile inside the School I engaged in a day-to-day struggle in my dual role; it was not merely a matter of the occasional disagreement behind closed doors but more often the daily intervention in routine matters to secure the maximum continuity of teaching, to counter the ever present tendency of a large school, for teachers, with self-indulgent standards, to regress to secondary modern attitudes and objectives. Fortunately the Heads of Departments, whose contribution to the success of the School was never properly acknowledged, understood and supported what I was trying to do. The Headmaster coped famously with the pressures, official and parental, but to the perceptive observer of the inside it could not be denied that the degree of autonomy I enjoyed over a wide degree of the organisation placed a strain on his natural temperamental assertiveness which had to find expression in ad hoc enterprises. Thus an anomalous situation developed in which many members of staff consulted me exclusively on matters which in any other school they would have referred to their headmaster, while visiting officials from County invariably engaged in confidential reference with the Headmaster, as was indeed as it should have been. The tension only arose from the circumstance that occasions occurred when they would have been better advised to consult the one of us who in practice exercised the power of decision and had the most intimate knowledge. When, as sometimes happened, I was called on to be present at a consultation with Officers from County Hall and or Governors, I found myself in the unenviable position of being witness to exchanges between parties whose utterances had one thing in common; complete ignorance of the matter at issue. It would not have done for me to speak.

This account of the peculiar nature of my role might well be attributed to conceit or exaggeration on my part. Yet after I had left the School I was visited by the young Head of Physics, Mr Clifford Stubbs. He had just succeeded in gaining promotion to a Head of Middle School in a large comprehensive. He told me that he had had many interviews for such posts. It had never failed to surprise him when, at such interviews, he met deputy headmasters, that their responsibilities and standing seemed restricted and lowly in comparison with what he had come to regard as the norm in his dealings with me at Hazelwick. The Head of Science, whose sequence of interviews in his prolonged and ultimately successful search for a job in his native Wales took him to even more schools, endorsed the comment. In the end, however, the acceptance of such an anomaly, whether in tacit silence in or ignorance of its existence, was bound to break down. For me the charade was exhausting. For the Headmaster it was frustrating. It broke down when I became too weary to defend those aspects of academic organisation which stood in the way of the Headmaster's plans for academic changes which I knew to be unworkable.

CHAPTER VI

AN INDIFFERENT QUALITY OF TEACHER

At the risk of inducing a sensation of surfeit among those for whom the seemingly endless debate on comprehensive schools has already gone on too long, I feel compelled to assert that, as a result of my experiences, not everything that needs to be said has yet been said. The case for preserving our grammar schools is self-evident to me, especially after discovering how bad some of our non-selective schools can be. The case for abolishing the divisiveness and finality of segregation by selection is equally cogent. The claim for better schools for less able pupils is not to be dismissed. What then remains to be said? Quite simply it is to assert that the quality of schooling depends firstly on the quality of the teaching, secondly on the quality of the teaching, and thirdly on the same. The extent to which this truism can be tacitly ignored by all parties to the debate becomes evident when one follows, as I have done, the public discussion and press publicity which a scheme of re-organisation can provoke when all the opportunities for consultation implied by Education Acts are exploited.

Robert Graves in his classic book on his experiences in the First World War, Goodbye to All That, recounts his recollection of an informal discussion among a group of officers awaiting their return to the trenches. How good was the British Army? The consensus of their opinions was that one third of its Divisions were first class and to be relied upon in all circumstances; one third was good for most of the time, but not unquestionably so under very adverse pressure; one third was, not to put too fine a point on it, just third rate, in other words not much good. My job of deploying the staff of a large comprehensive led me to form a similar judgement about teachers. I cannot escape the conclusion that much of the energy which is dissipated in the search for improvement through re-organisation, through administrative measures, through the advocacy of new techniques of teaching, would be much more profitably used in tackling what, when all is said and done, is the root problem in our system of schools, the indifferent quality of the supply of teachers. It did not shock or surprise me when a relative of my wife who became a teacher on giving up his commission in the Army, commented that he found a meeting of head teachers, in so far as the level of conversation was concerned, redolent of the Sergeants' mess. This implies no disparagement of sergeants, whose efficiency as soldiers had often impressed me. I sympathise, however, with the implication of the educational comparison. The impression one gains of the level of either the intelligence or culture of teachers as a whole depends upon the point in our system of schools that one encounters them. The conspiracy of silence over the extent of the gap between the quality of our best and of our worst teachers vitiates most public discussion of our schools. It is not so easy to overlook in a well-staffed comprehensive, where some of the more able sixth formers soon outstrip the tail-enders on the staff in both educational attainment and cultural awareness. I hasten to add that this circumstance never in my experience became a cause of overt embarrassment, largely because the non-academic qualities of persons as persons were appreciated, and the anomalies in intellectual abilities were never exposed by clumsy timetabling. The fact remains that the low level of entrance requirements upon which some Colleges of Education operate and the superficial level of knowledge they accept from student teachers should be the first concern of those who wish to reform our schools.

Just how unlikely such a reversal of priorities remains for the foreseeable future is apparent from contemporary ideas on the education of less able pupils. The prestigious Newsom Report, subtitled 'Half Our Future', was published soon after I was making my own discoveries about the problems of teaching less able pupils. Inevitably there was a conference organised by the County for teachers to consider and discuss this emotive and almost useless document. Among its hotch-potch of platitudes and vague suggestions there was one sensible recommendation: that teachers in deprived areas should be rewarded by higher salaries. I doubt if the differential envisaged by the authors of the report was of the magnitude necessary to affect the distribution of teaching ability, nor have I heard that it has been effectively implemented. As far as I was concerned the implication of the title of the Newsom Report – 'Half Our Future' – let alone the discursive series of propositions it contained, roused in me feelings of indignation and outrage. It was ironical that a reactionary academic such as myself should have found himself alone, in the welter of pseudo-enlightened chatter that the report evoked, in protesting against this relegation of one half – I still find it difficult to believe – one half of our secondary school pupils to the status of ineducability, to a substitute education consisting of improvised gimmickry, the dominant feature of which was that it should preclude sustained concentrated endeavour in any recognisable academic field of knowledge. It was a remedy born of desperation and incompetence. If you lack the insight and adaptability to teach traditional subjects or skills, then seek alleviation from frustration in devising interesting activities, no matter how transient the interest.

It was in my third year as a comprehensive teacher that I began to get to grips with this notoriously intractable problem of the low-ability classes whose difficulties are increased by the approach of the prospect of leaving school and earning money. After I had become satisfied that our precious and hard-won grammar school intake was well launched, that the uncreamed status of the school was secure, I gave myself a teaching timetable that consisted almost entirely of lessons with every form in the third year. There were at that time eight such forms, and the degree of streaming which I inherited from the secondary modern era was unrefined by any banding. Thus by teaching the same History syllabus to all levels of ability I was able to study the problems of differing abilities in what was almost a controlled experiment. The most important discovery was that if one maintained the same pressure of work on all classes, and evinced the same degree of interest and expectation, one was rewarded with the same response. It was, of course, very evident that the pace of work and scope of the syllabus had to be progressively modified with diminishing ability. Yet the modification had to consist in the range of the syllabus and not, as is attempted by the authors of so many text-books for secondary modern schools, by a thinning out of the material so that the least able pupils were those who had to make sense of a desiccated string of generalisations. The contrary technique proved most effective, that of increasing the depth of study, the imparting of a closely related body of detailed facts, as the capacity for conceptual thinking declined.

I must be honest and confess that I was a failure with the least able class, the lower of the two comprising the remedial classes of the third year. I conceded the autonomy of the teachers of the Remedial Department. The main difficulty was language register. Despite my great endeavour to simplify my vocabulary according to the ability level of each class, it seemed to me that this particular handicap almost precluded separate subject syllabuses. The allocation of seven remedial teachers to cover the basic teaching of literacy and numeracy to the eight remedial forms, the two most backward in each of the four years, proved very successful. There was a steady movement of pupils, usually one or two at a time, from the remedial forms upwards into the main body of the School. The greatest handicap suffered by these pupils, as far as teachers were concerned, was the appointment of inadequate personalities from last-minute applications. There always seemed to be one weak member in an otherwise dedicated and competent team. This was, of course true of other Departments. In the latter cases, however, the damage to the pupils could be minimised by the limited number of lessons each week which such teachers were given with any one class. In the Remedial Department one teacher was allocated for about twenty-five lessons a week with a particular form to permist intimate knowledge of all pupils to be developed.

With the exception of the remedial pupils I experienced no difficulty in teaching the same syllabus, appropriately modified, to all forms in the third year. Much has been said about the importance of the teachers getting to know their pupils well. I wish to stress the other side of the picture. It proved an inestimable benefit to the development of the School that all the pupils in one year got to know the Deputy Headmaster well. The mutual confidence that developed was reflected in morale and behaviour. As for the pernicious nonsense about half of them being unable to follow an orthodox curriculum, this proved nothing but an indictment of the lack of imagination and intensity of so much teaching. Three of the more rumbustious boys in the fifth stream of that third year turned up later on in my O level History class and gained grade five passes. In this they were much encouraged in their aspirations by our vigorous Head of English, who had stretched their minds and disciplined their energies by including them in the cast of the School production of Henry IV, Part I.

Such, however, was the acclaim with which the Newsom report was generally received that it was unavoidable that the School had to show some response to it. A meeting was called by the Headmaster at which Departments were invited to submit ideas for a Newsom curriculum. What emerged was a collection of subjects reflecting the variety of interests of those teachers who were inveigled into participation in the scheme. There were lessons in guitar playing, the dismemberment of motor cycles, camping and camp cooking, play acting, cookery for boys and so forth. The timetable allowed for the rotation of small groups and a lavish provision of teachers. The Headmaster was overheard in jocular mood making the claim over the phone to County that, as always, the School was in the lead, the first to set up a Newsom Department. The post of Head of the Newsom Department was incorporated into the structure of teaching posts carrying an extra allowance. The post and the allowance became a permanent part of the staffing structure. The Newsom curriculum hardly lasted a year. A particularly vociferous critic was a member of the kitchen staff who demanded to know why she had seen her son shovelling coke outside the boiler houses.

It was not until 1966 that I finally timetabled a curriculum for a low-ability form which gave effect to my convictions and which embodied the experience of teaching such forms in previous years. The unique feature of the 1966 scheme was that I was planned to begin in the first year and to be sustained with as great a degree of continuity as possible for four years with the same pupils. The choice of the first year form for this experiment was fortuitous. I was within one or two lessons of completing the timetable which at that time consisted of over three thousand lessons a week. It seemed impossible to fill the final gaps in the timetable of a class designated F3Z, for by that time the number of forms in the first year had risen to twelve, and these were streamed into three bands plus the Remedial Department. Form F3Z was thus just above the remedial forms. It was at the level at which one could anticipate a steady deterioration in interest, morale and behaviour over the four years preceding the statutory leaving age. I found that I could only complete the timetable of this form by filling the gaps myself.

After meeting these children in the classroom I was so impressed by their liveliness and tractability that I decided forthwith to amend their timetable in such a way that it gave effect to two ideas: the number of teachers was reduced and those who agreed to join me in the experiment were as highly qualified as possible in the academic sense. The aim was to stand Newsom on its head. The curriculum was to be traditional and the teaching as intensive as possible. A very outstanding and dedicated young woman, Mrs Petch, undertook their English, and, as soon as it was possible to make the timetable alterations, their French and Maths. Dr Jensen, the vigorous Head of Chemistry, taught the three natural sciences; I taught History, Geography and Religious Knowledge. The remainder of the curriculum, Music, Art and Craft, was not allocated to especially selected teachers. Thus nine academic subjects were taught to this below-average form by three highly qualified teachers for whom advanced sixth form work was a more obvious pre-occupation, but all dedicated to the proposition that morale and behaviour of a low-ability form would be sustained at its initial level of high expectation by intensive teaching.

Unlike some teachers who have interested themselves in this problem of maintaining the interest of the early school-leaver, I tried to resist the temptation to publicise a hypothesis as if it were a proved solution. This happens all too often in teaching. Any novel method which provides an escape from formal teaching will produce an initial success, simply by virtue of the response to novelty. Almost any unconventional method will succeed if put into effect by an enthusiast who originates it. Experiments in novel methods of teaching leave a trail of abandoned schemes and demoralised pupils, largely because of an almost total absence of scientific appraisal. The intensity of the antipathy among those who are responsible for training non-graduate teachers to formal teaching is exemplified by the following passage from a book by a lecturer in a famous teaching training institution:

'How can we hope that any young people will in schooltime engage in any worthwhile creative thinking if they are never allowed to brood, to stay at something a little longer, to move on in apparent restlessness to minor chores while the ground is fallow for negative capability?

'Again how do we explain a youth time arbitrarily divided into spasms of thirty, forty, or forty-five minutes, punctuated by the clanging of bells, and often followed by a massive flocking in and out of corridors? How do we reconcile this planned incoherence with our knowledge of the different rhythms of learning different individuals have, of their different degrees of P factor (perseveration, mercifully permitted to be amoral, unlike those hardened virtues, persistence and perseverance)?

'Again is it really a requirement of equality of educational opportunity in a mass society that young people should have to prove themselves equal to sitting down periodically in a room with a clock in order to inform their elders of familiar facts?'

(*Young Lives at Stake* by Charity James, Collins 1968)

Although this quotation tells us nothing about how to run a large school, its tendentiousness tells us much about the prejudices of its author. Children will brood whether we like it or not, particularly if their relationships with their families or their peers are presenting them with problems. Unimpeded restlessness usually leads to truancy, which in turn can lead to shoplifting or child pregnancy. As for the choice of words in this intensely felt polemic against conventional schooling – 'spasm' for interval, 'flocking' for walking, 'planned incoherence' for arrangements for avoiding chaos, 'hardened' as a pejorative term characterising 'virtues', it is impossible to read such a diatribe and to regard it as a serious and detached contribution to thinking about teaching.

Yet the sentiments expressed are typical of the new orthodoxy. It became a matter of weary acceptance by experienced and thoughtful teachers that every batch of student teachers sent to us for teaching practice by Colleges of Education would ask to begin by breaking up their classes into groups and setting work in the form of projects. The point of such methods was never made clear, and could only be taken as symptomatic of this deep rooted desire to eschew formality. I have seen project work undertaken with complete success by very experienced and gifted teachers. To expect students to manipulate a situation the strangeness of which was to some classes an immediate source of tension seemed to me a certain recipe for the confusion and disorder that inevitably ensued. The futility of these perennial masochistic exercises was redolent of the generalship of the First World War, the repetitive resort on an ever increasing scale of tactics which always failed. On one occasion a student gathered the class around the blackboard for an English lesson which, in order to maximise pupil participation, was to consist of word building. The first boy began the exercise by writing the letter F. The exercise took its predictable course. The next boy added the letter U. The hilarity which this experiment in teaching provoked might have passed unnoticed had it not caused such a convulsion of merriment that one boy fell from his perch on a desk and cut open his head. An entry on an accident report gave the incident more publicity than was intended. I hope the student recovered from the avoidable setback.

For most of my time as the Deputy Head I had the responsibility for supervising the work of postgraduate students in teacher training from a nearby university. Though on the whole this proved a profitable arrangement for all concerned, there was sometimes an initial difficulty to be overcome in the form of a prejudice among some students manifest in their tolerant condescension towards teachers of my age group. I recollect how one such student momentarily reduced me to speechlessness by his contribution at a seminar, delivered with an air of patronising superiority: 'But your job is to interest the children.' I reflected that in ignoring the obvious and the platitudinous I was overestimating the sophistication of innocence. Courtesy inhibited a rejoinder, but mentally I awarded a black mark to the institution that purveyed such truisms as having the weight of professional insights.

The experiment with F3Z to give effect to our belief that an intense pressure of formal work on a traditional curriculum, albeit adjusted to the ability of the pupils, and an overt display of intense interest and expectation was as much the formula for success with lower-ability forms as with top streams, was not proclaimed as a panacea. Indeed it was not proclaimed at all. For it was, after all, an experiment. A hypothesis to be tested. Such detachment is, I regret to say, not typical of educational theory or practice. However, we proceeded so untypically that many of the staff were unaware of our enterprise, and remained so. Yet we began with one firmly held conviction: that specious schemes and projects designed to give effect to the defeatism of Newsom were recipes for a progressive erosion of morale from an excited readiness to work to a sullen indifference to schooling altogether. Not that fourth year leavers were, by 1966, a notable problem at Hazelwick. Since 1962 when I took over the timetabling I had always put myself and the Senior Mistress, Miss Anslow, and later her successor, Mrs Jones, and any other of the more able teachers on the timetables of what were deemed to be the most difficult forms. I made known my view that only the best teachers were entitled to teach the least enthusiastic classes. As for pupils who were known to be leaving as soon as entitled to do so, it was firm policy not to segregate them or to react to their intention in any way, apart from providing the best Youth Employment Advice available. What was new about the F3Z experiment was the intention to commit to it a purposeful team of teachers and to keep them involved with the same pupils for, if possible, their whole school career. The experiment was confined to one form because, even if there had been available the number of teachers of high qualifications, perception and dedication to extend it to other forms, the distortion of the timetable of sixth forms together with the disruption of setting systems, would have been hard to justify for the sake of an experiment.

The results of our limited endeavours were interesting when viewed honestly and with detachment. The first two years were an unqualified success. The fact that homework was set with unfailing regularity, and, what is more important, always marked with attention to detail, was rewarded as we had anticipated by high morale. In 1968 I was sufficiently encouraged to write a letter to the Times Educational Supplement, which appeared under the title 'Reappraising Newsom'.

'Sir – I wonder if any other of your readers would agree that perhaps the time has come for a reappraisal of Newsom, both the report and the concept of a type of pupil for which it purports to show concern.

'After eight years in a comprehensive school with timetables in which lessons with so-called Newsom pupils have featured largely, I would like to suggest that the curricular content of the report, with its implicit invitation to substitute informal group activities, constitutes a dangerous tendency to educational apartheid, all the more sinister for being presented under the guise of progress. While one may concede that informal group activities, visits and extra-mural work generally may be a great improvement on sterile and tedious classroom work, the case has yet to be made that it is an advance on good stimulating teaching of a more orthodox kind.

'My experience has led me to a conviction that the below average child is too readily regarded as a subject for novel experiments which lead to curricular deprivation and an increased separation from the non-Newsom child. May I suggest the alternative and simple remedy, namely, the use of above average teachers, particularly high calibre general subject teachers, or teachers able to teach groups of related subjects with enthusiasm. To teach with more awareness of pupil reaction, to teach a little more slowly, more patiently, with more persistence, and above all, more cheerfully, may seem to some to be a formula of unattractive banality. In practice such teachers are now so rare as to constitute an elite of comparable status to that of the third year sixth form scholarship teacher.

'The current issue of 'Where' gives ample expression to cogent arguments of those who see salvation in unstreaming. Though not fully convinced of the case for unstreaming, I suggest that it may have an added virtue, one which has not, as far as I am aware been claimed for it. If by less streaming we are forced to break down the barriers set up by Newsom, a barrier in some respects more final than that of 11 plus selection, then let us hope for all success to the destreamers.

L F Moore
Deputy Headmaster,
Hazelwick School

Not for the first or last time did I await a response in vain to a published letter of mine. The concept of a Newsom pupil remains part of contemporary orthodoxy. I like to think that in practice its sterility is leading to its tacit consignment to oblivion.

It is significant that those of us who committed ourselves to this enterprise with form F3Z had no common view on the matter of classroom discipline, on formality as opposed to informality between teachers and pupils. The common factor in our work with these pupils was a belief in the moral effect of hard purposeful work and a sustained interest in its results. I had already reached the age at which I was becoming increasingly allergic to noise. Yet the fact that my lessons were conducted on the basis of a rule that no one speaks while work is in progress, except to me, did not inhibit the development of a relationship of mutual respect and trust. I could not conceive of any circumstance in which I could have been induced to use a cane or any form of corporal punishment on a boy in that class. On the other hand, as my punishment book shows, I did cane boys very occasionally when they had been sent to me by student or probationer teachers, whose desperation over the deliberate and malevolent disruption of their lessons by lazy and resilient boys was all too evident.

A proper regard for truth, for complete objectivity in the assessment of the success of one's own ideas is no more a feature of pedagogic debate than it is of political discussions. Remembering that the precise object of the exercise was to maintain the initial attitudes of acceptance and aspiration in a group of pupils whose academic and innate abilities more usually led to anything ranging from indifference to overt hostility to school by the time they had reached the fourth year, the experiment was a success and a vindication of the ideas upon which it was based. This claim has to be qualified carefully in one or two respects. The success was notably more marked in respect of behaviour and morale than academic attainment. The latter was difficult to assess owing to a development that had not been part of the original plan. The intention to keep the class together as a closely observed group foundered on the very success of the commitment to intense formal teaching. One by one a few pupils emerged as pace setters and as more responsive to teaching than the average for the form. They were promoted out of the class, though with great reluctance on the part of their teachers, because they had begun to evince the discontent of boredom, and, in one case, a sense of victimisation at denial of promotion. Similarly there were three pupils who joined the class at different times, promoted from the remedial department. It was significant that two of these were girls whose 'promotion' owed less to academic attainment than to the fact they were becoming problem pupils, and F3Z was earning a reputation of being a problem-solving group. In the third year another girl was admitted as a transfer from another school, where her career had been chequered and disaffected.

The departure of the most able pupils and the admission of others who had already learned how to plague teachers beyond endurance might well have produced a form of fourth year leavers with the normal tendency to dodge work or lapse into sporadic truancy. That this did not occur is largely due to the influence of the form teacher Rhianon Patch, a personality of great charm and high intelligence. Her perseverance and concern for her pupils reflected a great strength of character. As I had written in my letter to The Times Educational Supplement, teachers of this calibre are rare. Mrs Patch resigned to have a child. I do not know how she evaluates her exceptional endeavours as a teacher in retrospect.

Another circumstance that complicated any purely academic assessment was the fragmentation of the form in those subjects which were options for CSE. By the time the class reached its fourth year, I had relinquished the Geography and RK, as it would have been a deprivation to deny pupils specialist teaching at this stage. Thus I met only those pupils who opted for History, for which subject they had to combine with pupils from two other forms. The options to History were Physics and Typing. All the girls chose Typing. I had in fact set up this particular option in the anticipation that they would do so. It had long been clear to me that although I obtained exceptional results as a History teacher with boys, I was not very successful with girls of below-average ability. In this context I am using the term 'below average' without qualification. I invariably found that girls in this category were at best assiduous and docile, but without the imagination to achieve any sense of the reality of events outside their own experience or related to their own immediate pre-occupations. In this connection I should perhaps stress that I never regarded project work, the drawing of costumes or cutting out pictures from one book to stick in another book as constituting teaching or learning. History is essentially something to be read, though recent television programmes have increased the possibilities of the development of historical perspectives visually. I hasten to add, as it were in parenthesis, that I deplore any discussion of subjects, such as History, in isolation from the rest of the curriculum. It is an occupational failing for specialist teachers to try to justify any subject in isolation. Be that as it may, I saw little of the girls of F3Z after the third year.

Before I dismiss them from the narrative I think it worth making reference to what, I suspect, is an interesting and significant feature of their relationship with the boys. It is usually asserted, in discussion of co-education, that girls excel academically in the first two years of secondary schooling, after which they are equalled or overtaken by the boys. This was not true in my experience of below average girls in general. In the case of F3Z, the manifestations of temperament, in some cases of simple temper, was far more a feature of relationships of the girls among themselves than those of the boys. Indeed, the latter tended to hold a patronising and disparaging view of the girls as being 'silly' and lacking common sense. To do justice to the girls, their seemingly endless capacity for intriguing against one another, for ganging up against a non-conforming member of their sex, were much more in evidence after the admission to the class of the late entrants. One of these was given to tantrums of such violence that she was sent, as was the routine in such cases, for analysis at the Child Guidance Clinic. Again, as was usual in such cases, the report from the psychiatrist told us nothing we did not know already. In the end I discovered that the most fruitful therapy for this child was to let her spend a day or two in the Prefects' Room. I explained to the girl prefects what was known about the family circumstances of this child. It was suggested by her form teacher, though not by the psychologist, that her place in her family, a large one of eight siblings, might have caused her to have been weaned prematurely. In any case we asked the prefects to look after her for a few days and to show her as much affectionate interest as possible. The girl, whose tantrums made her unmanageable and who had walked out of school, defying even the Headmaster, became sweet tempered and tractable. The Prefects' Room, however, could not provide a substitute for lessons and the nearest we came to solving this child's problems was a timetable by means of which she took some lessons with one form and some with another, the allocation being so arranged to give her as many lessons as possible with men teachers, and as few as possible with those girls who seemed to trigger off her paranoia.

There was one other girl from the original F3Z who became a problem in the fourth year. She was found to be guilty of petty theft. Her parents refused to visit the School to discuss the matter on the grounds that it was none of their business what the girl did at school. We discovered that they had encouraged her to defy teachers and walk out of school if windows were not shut at her request when she was at junior school.

The remainder of the girls in F3Z rewarded our exceptional attention by reaching the statutory leaving age without developing an indifference to school work or any overt symptoms of antipathy to being at school. Some of them remained for the extra voluntary year to take CSE. On the other hand the whole experiment gave some indication of the limits as well as the benefits of formal education. Although the intensity of the teaching effort, the continuity of the relationship between teachers and pupils, and the dedicated personal interest of their form teacher seemed to keep these particular boys and girls in a trustful relationship with their teachers, the influence of the latter did not appear to have much effect on what one can only regard as the behaviour derived from the cultural background. This was most apparent in their attitudes to one another, particularly in the case of the girls. There was an ever changing pattern of cliques among the girls which seemed to be formed solely for the purpose of persecuting one of their number whose behaviour did not meet with the approval of the dominating personalities. Fortunately these malevolent combinations were short lived, and those who suffered from them enjoyed participation in turn in another exercise of intolerance. The emotional outbursts to which these primitive animosities could give rise were of a violence that surprised me on the one occasion in which I came upon the scene. Usually these schoolgirl feuds were not apparent in the classroom. Unfortunately a teacher who had been listed to cover a lesson for an absent colleague failed to read the staff notice-board and the class was left unattended. I discovered it in a state of uproar towards the end of the lesson. One girl was weeping because another had pulled out some of her hair. I cannot recall the alleged cause of this incident, except that it was one of those which caused me to be grateful for the experience and aid of one of the lady teachers of the old secondary modern days.

Our endeavours with F3Z were more successful with the boys, perhaps because there were no late entrants to the class among them. There was one who would certainly have become a troublesome bully-boy in the third or fourth year had he been in a less favoured form. His home was bereft of any educational advantage, and his father had left his mother to cope with his upbringing in which she was well intentioned but overindulgent. He grew into a strong big boy who played a rough game of rugger. In the fourth year he showed signs of wanting to challenge the School. His homework was not done unless he was detained at school to do it. He sought the company of boys of bad reputation in other forms. Yet it was significant that at the end of four years in F3Z he failed totally to recruit a following in that form where the values of the School which had been so readily accepted in the first year remained undisturbed for the whole four years of the experiment.

There was one other boy who failed to respond, who became lazy and listless. His case presented us with an intractable problem which was at root medical. He had been badly injured as a child when he had run in front of a car. Normally this sort of information was recorded on a 'Disability List', a confidential document compiled from information from parents and junior schools with the arrival of each new intake. I was also sorry that the parents, who came to see the Headmaster more than once, never got as far as consultation with those of us who were so deeply involved in teaching the boy.

I don't know what depth of intimacy and length of unbroken observation of a single group of boys and girls would be deemed sufficient basis for making generalisation by a lecturer in education. Knowing that it is possible to be appointed a lecturer in Education at a College of Education without ever having taught at all and with minimal academic qualifications, I count myself well qualified to theorise. Yet, although a graduate in History, I am by temperament disinclined to regard either the findings of my own or anyone else in teaching as having the validity of a truly scientific investigation. What amazes me is the way the expansion of our 'education' system has attracted numbers of so-called experts who will propagate, either explicitly or by implication, their ideas about teaching as if they had been tested with the thoroughness of an engineering process about to be committed to the production line. Would that it were so. It is, of course, not so. Anyone in this country can be an expert on teaching, like the man who fooled us that he had a degree in Economics, then left us to become an educational consultant. I hesitate to join this ragtime crew who exploit the credulous.

The four years with F3Z, like my seven years with the grammar school intake of 1961, taught me a great deal. Both experiences hardened my conviction that pupils are grateful for thorough painstaking teaching, free from diversions into cul de sacs of pedagogic 'mucking about'. Yet I would be less than honest if I did not recount that all the trouble we took to teach F3Z, as much as we could in four years, did not have any effect on their individual decisions to remain at school for a fifth year. At least half of them left as soon as they reached the statutory leaving age of fifteen. It was abundantly clear that their decisions in this matter were made by the attitude of parents, by elder brothers or sisters who were earning good money after leaving school at fifteen, or by the influence and example of friends. It was of no avail to point out that with the raising of the school-leaving age they would be the last entrants to the labour force not to have had five years of secondary schooling. In the School as a whole the proportion of pupils remaining voluntarily had been high for some years. The fact that less than a half remained from a form that was placed just above the remedial forms, but below eight other forms in terms of eleven plus scores should surprise no one. What struck me as very significant was the way they compared with pupils from the stream immediately above them whom they joined in their fourth year to form classes in option subjects. In class work there seemed nothing to choose between the attainment of those I had taught of the previous three years and those from the other forms in the lower CSE band. It was only when I set homework which called for concentration, and reference to textbooks, that those boys who came from F3Z emerged as the pace setters. They went on working against inclination and circumstance. Morally they were a superior product of schooling.

It was two years later that I met two former members of F3Z who had left school at the end of the fourth year, accepting the advice of their parents and rejecting that of their teacher. In the course of conversation they commented on their schooling. They were critical. They had learnt nothing at school. I was not unduly impressed by this judgement. If they had remained for another year and taken no exam, they would have made the same comment. Parents whose insistence on a leaving exam led to the CSE exam were right. I knew that these boys could have achieved a fair range of CSE passes. Those who did remain and took home a fistful of Certificates did not claim to have learnt nothing at school. In this same chance conversation one of the lads said something which pleased me more than he could have guessed. He told me about his girlfriend. It seems that she was still at school, a girls' grammar school of high repute, and was taking A levels.

When pressed to state my position in respect of academic aims in a comprehensive school, I had always indicated as my guiding ideal a curriculum in which there was graduation of difficulty but no total divisiveness in content. I wanted, I used to say, to make it possible for a pupil from the lower streams to marry happily with one from the higher streams. An unlikely outcome, I agree. Even so it pleased me to think of my young friend from F3Z going steady with his girl from the High School sixth form.

The success of the four-year experiment in trying to teach, as distinct from merely entertain or interest, a class of less able boys and girls, of deliberately swimming against the tide, like much else that was achieved at Hazelwick, remains a source of satisfaction to me, diminished only by the knowledge that swimming against the tide deprives an endeavour of permanency or recognition. Yet my most treasured testimonial came in the form of a letter from the brilliant young woman who had acted as form teacher to these children for the first three years of our enterprise. Indeed, without her I might well have faltered in my purpose. After I had resigned I was delighted to hear from her.

> 'Only this week I heard of your having left Hazelwick… It is much too late to say so now, but I would like you to know what a positive strong influence for good I felt you to be in the School and in my development as a teacher there… Your humane, rigorous, skilful handling of pupils is something I shall never forget. One of the marks of a great teacher is that his pupils never forget him or what, in the widest sense, they learned from him. I feel sure that many young people whom you taught will feel, as I do, that you have been a key figure in their development… I am not alone in remembering Frank Moore, teacher extraordinary, with gratitude and affection.'

Such praise from such a source does much to counteract the sadness of knowing that after my departure, along with so many of the stalwarts who supported me, the phrase makers, the facile optimists for whom no difficulty cannot be soon obscured by the panacea of discussion, will soon permeate the activities of yet another school. 'Humane, skilful, rigorous…' I could not have stated with such succinctness the character toward which I aspired, albeit sometimes so ineffectively.

CHAPTER VII

PARENTAL EXPECTATIONS

It was never made clear to the Headmaster or myself what sort of school we were expected to develop as a result of re-organisation, except that it should be such as to win the same esteem with parents as had hitherto been accorded to the Grammar School. In temperament and training the Headmaster and I differed in almost every respect. Yet in the matter of an acute consciousness of parental expectations we had a common ground which enabled us to confer daily as a matter of routine. A recent leading article in a national newspaper discussed the issue of comprehensive schools as consisting in a choice between two types: the grammar school made comprehensive, and the secondary modern comprehensive. It argued, not without reason, that the latter invariably fell pathetically short of the academic standards and attainments of the former. The degree to which I enjoyed autonomy in academic organisation enabled us to belie the generalisation. This meant a transformation of an unusual degree, and I settled down for a long hard slog. Hazelwick, far from providing the basis of an easy transition, had been a secondary modern school that suffered much from the hostility of the parents of its neighbourhood. Against this must be set the freedom we enjoyed from guidance from the County.

The dubious reputation of Hazelwick before re-organisation may well have stemmed from the fact that, as the first secondary school to be built for the New Town, its first few intakes consisted largely of older pupils unwillingly transferred from all over the decaying areas of London as their parents moved with the factories to the Industrial Estate. At one time there were as many as two hundred schools contributing to the flow of new entrants to Hazelwick, most of them nearer the end of their schooling than the beginning. A less resilient man than the Headmaster would not have survived those difficult years before

1960. When I arrived at Hazelwick in that year I soon recognised a few boys whose obstreperous behaviour at Ifield Grammar School had been more than its headmaster could tolerate. As a secondary modern, and later as a comprehensive, Hazelwick did not enjoy this advantage of being able to relegate its difficult members to another institution. It is an admission I cannot avoid making that one of the first decisions following re-organisation was not to expend too much energy in any attempts to effect a major transformation in the aspirations and attitudes of the disaffected elements in the third and fourth years. Fortunately, from 1960 onwards the majority of pupils entering the school were first formers from the neighbourhood junior schools.

For the first year or two of our partnership, the Headmaster continued to think and behave as a secondary modern teacher; I never wavered in my grammar school priorities. Later, as the headmaster of a comprehensive and as teacher representative on the Education Committee, his judgement seemed to concur increasingly with mine, particularly about the work of young teachers. For example, differences, such as over the best method of conveying criticism to a colleague, were a source of tension; outsiders such as the Director of Education and his Assistants never even began to understand the prolonged ordeal of self-abnegation they had so deliberately inflicted on both of us. The Headmaster's frustrations resulting from my appointment were to some extent mitigated by his continued access to the Education Officers at County Hall. As for me I do not know whether the latter wished to forget the extent of the obligations they had placed on me. Their behaviour was such as to suggest that they wished to forget I existed.

It might be supposed that as an ex-grammar-school master of forty-five I was so immutably conditioned that the objectives towards which I strove were a foregone conclusion. Not so. Long before I abandoned the stable and familiar routine of the grammar school I had become uneasy about its limitations. I was already aware of the inward-looking pre-occupation of many grammar school teachers with the aim of producing in their pupils the same attitudes and values that had governed their own lives when sixth formers. Mark you: they could have done worse. Yet to produce good sixth formers of the traditional pattern is an inadequate aim when it becomes the over-riding aim. The main advantage of grammar schools over secondary modern, in this matter of objectives, was that in the former they were well defined and clearly understood in academic terms. It surprised me to discover how far this was untrue of a secondary modern school of the fifties, and the extent to which this left the field open for charlatans on the periphery and in the underworld of the system to mislead bewildered teachers with their unproved hypotheses. On my arrival at Hazelwick, among comments from the secondary modern staff were expressions of relief that at last they knew where they were going.

My sympathy with the aspirations of parents predisposed me to adopt a traditional curriculum and methods in which the pressure of work was as finely adjusted to the ability of classes as possible, and as such to be the source of higher morale. My recollections of my conceit as a young teacher strengthened my sympathy with parents. The interest of teachers in their pupils is intense, but of necessity it is ephemeral. It is difficult for the beginner to realise that the boy or girl who occupies a place of primacy in their present concern will so quickly become one whose name it is difficult to remember. On those occasions when I had to try and resolve conflicts between parents and children, I made what some may regard as morbid reference to the possibility of accidents. I added that, from my observation, the sense of loss following the death of a pupil, however intense at the time, was of limited duration at school. If grief is the measure of concern, the pretensions of a school or teachers to dictate the outcome of schooling with total disregard for the parents, is an obscene impertinence.

These views were re-inforced by my adherence to the doctrine that a teacher has the obligation of a freely signed contract. The ability of men to keep their word, their acceptance of the restraints implicit in their contractual obligation, is the basis of civilisation. The upshot of such a premise is the creation of a school which is in most respects orthodox, albeit progressive in the refinement of its organisation and provisions. The Headmaster and I thus were agreed in discomfiting the teacher who regarded the classroom as a place for constant inconsequential chit-chat by which he or she deluded themselves that something significant was happening. As a Head of a History Department in a grammar school I had imposed on myself the discipline of reading a daily stint in order to familiarise myself with all new published books on my period. Gradually my knowledge increased beyond the demands of the A level syllabus, and was reflected in a predilection for study in depth. I became wedded to a belief in the slow but inexorable effect of uninterrupted assiduous teaching, the water continuously wearing away the stone. At the same time I knew the value of being able to expatiate on the interesting details. It delighted me to discover that the effectiveness of teaching in depth and the avoidance of superficial generalisations was even more a key to success with low-ability classes, so long as care was taken to ensure that vocabulary and concepts did not go beyond the limits of their understanding.

My appointment as Senior Academic Master preceded the departure of the Deputy Head of the secondary modern School for a headship by an interval of five terms. This was a happy circumstance which enabled me to proceed in the matter of academic changes with wariness. Not till my second year did I begin to evolve a related system of courses, options, and examinations, and a system of promotions and transfers between classes. My period as an onlooker was not wasted. The institution of compulsory homework and the steady pressure to step up the work done by pupils, as distinct from their listening to teacher, had already begun before I took over the Deputy Headship. I followed these steps by establishing a routine of examinations and reports to parents which were staggered in such a way as to obviate the run-down in teaching towards the end of each term. This was a feature of my grammar school experience I was determined to eliminate. Teaching was to continue to the last day of each term. For example, fourth year exams were timed for the last week of the Easter term and arranged so as not to interfere with the continuance of lessons by the rest of the School. Decisions about school-leaving and careers could then be discussed at a Parents' Evening early in the Summer term. An exam for third forms in those subjects from which they had to choose as GCE or CSE options was similarly held at a time apart from yearly school exams, to be followed likewise by consultation with parents. At the end of the Summer term, after the completion of CSE and GCE, there remained only the less prolonged exams for first and second years, the non-option subjects only for the third years and exams for the lower sixth. Since the Mock GCE and CSE exams had to be held in January and February, the Autumn term was the only time free from exams. On the other hand, apart from pupils taking CSE, none took more than one examination a year. The staggered timing of exams and reports, and of the Parents' Evenings that followed them, caused some staff to grumble at what seemed to them as an unending round of such chores. I think it was mainly the younger ones who tended to forget that their burdens were significantly lightened by eschewing the customary end-of-term frenzy of examinations for the whole School, followed by frantic writing of reports and neglect of teaching.

The Heads of Departments aided me famously in the achievement of more intensive and continuous teaching. The Head of Maths, Michael Moore, also came to my assistance in his last years at the School before he became a headmaster in relieving me of the major exam administration in the Summer term, enabling me to concentrate on the timetable for next year. Heads of Departments also dealt with the problem of books. Inflation caused targets for expenditure to recede continuously. Matters were not helped by the failure of the County at the time of re-organisation to appreciate that the books previously acquired by the secondary modern school were useless as a nucleus for a stock on which to base the closely integrated courses of a comprehensive school. There had been many purchases before re-organisation of half-sets of books, the assumption being, incredible as it may now seem, that the main business of learning consisted of listening to teacher, with the issue of books to be shared by each pair of pupils to be regarded as a very secondary device. The problem of allocating money to subjects was dealt with at a meeting summoned each year by the Headmaster of all Heads of Departments. In the last resort agreement was reached because of the professional readiness of one department to surrender some of its allocation to another department following thorough discussion. This evidence of ability of the Heads of Departments to reach a compromise where their interests conflicted deserves praise.

My first timetable was made when I became Deputy Head. The number of pupils on the roll was then just over a thousand, and I was able to enjoy the intellectual exercise. The sixth form consisted of four boys only, the first ever at the School to be timetabled for A levels, products of the old secondary modern school who had been given six years to gain their O levels. The energy of the Head of Science, Dr Llewellyn, took them through to A levels in Physics; the new Head of Maths, Michael Moore, undertook to take them to A level in Applied Maths and Pure Maths. Officially the sixth form was planned to emerge five years later, but by that time I was timetabling for a school of sixteen hundred, with twenty-two different subject combinations, free from timetable clashes, in A level subjects. By then the options at O level provided over two hundred and fifty permutations of combinations of subjects for fourth and fifth year GCE classes.

My predecessor bequeathed me my timetabling equipment. I never discovered among the various devices that, with the growth of large schools, were marketed by commercial concerns to serve as timetabling aids any that were as good as his board covered with one-inch tapes to provide pockets into which little tickers representing teachers and lessons could be slotted. The method by which these were placed on the board contained built-in safeguards against errors. The board was primarily a device for working out the timetable. After it was completed the timetables of a hundred teachers and fifty forms had to be copied in duplicate, and it was these rather than the board that served as reference sources when someone wished to know the whereabouts of a pupil, a teacher, or a class. At first I used to call on the help of a secretary to read through with me all these timetables to check against copying errors, to avoid a clash of classes or teachers trying to enter the same room during the first week of term. Later I was able to estimate the probable number of such errors as being too few to justify taking up the time of a secretary for a whole week of the summer 'holidays'. It took less time to allow the discrepancies to emerge during the first week of term and to amend the errors in question there and then.

In the matter of timetabling, as in most things, I preferred to work on my own. I know teachers who bought and read books on timetabling. I never found one that seemed to me to go beyond the obvious. The best help I had was the advice of my predecessor on the sequence of subjects to be adopted. Although I began by trying to collect as much information as possible from Heads of Departments about their preferences as to the number and distribution of lessons in their own subjects, I enjoyed the freedom of working alone, the freedom to seek the ideal solution without the painful restraint of committee work. I had by now prescriptions for achieving an ideal distribution of lessons for each form. For example it seemed to me unfortunate if a double or treble lesson on the games field should fall on the same day as a double or treble Craft or Art lesson, as this would prevent the daily Maths, English and French lessons from taking place, and result in one or more days when the class had nothing but a bunch of academic classroom lessons. One had to keep an eye on all sorts of esoteric considerations, such as the incidence of PE lessons and Games, leaving the necessary intervals for mother to wash the prescribed garments.

Let it be stated unequivocally that two visits were made by computer programmers and achieved nothing. After I had outlined the complexities of the option systems and the refinements I required in distribution of lessons for both pupils and staff, they departed. They did not re-appear or make so bold as to proffer help. I have heard it said that a computer could achieve a seventy-five per cent provision of timetable requirements. This might do for some schools. But when I insisted that account be taken of the incidence of sixth form private study, in order to place as many sixth formers in lessons towards the end of the day, when their capacity for private study would be wearing thin, I realised I was on my own. In any case the constantly changing shape of the School made a computerised timetable uneconomic. By the shape of the School I mean the number of forms of first year children entering each year. As it varied year by year, from eight to as many as twelve, and never reached even a forecast of stability, the timetable for each year was a new one. The fact that we adopted a policy of providing options as demanded by pupils, this factor alone would have prevented a repeat timetable, even if the distribution of boys and girls in each year had become stabilised. A further complication was the sporadic increase in buildings. The increase in permanent buildings was always welcome. Unfortunately such provision rarely co-incided with the steady growth of the number of boys and girls on the roll of the school. The discrepancy was met by the addition of hutted classrooms. Yet when numbers started to fall as a result of the raising of the age of transfer from junior schools from eleven to twelve plus, the removal of huts seemed somehow equally ill timed.

The West Sussex handbook of its schools could thus be very misleading if the phrase 'purpose-built' was taken too literally. There were six huts at the time of re-organisation in 1960. Subsequently the number rose to a maximum of eighteen. After 1970 huts were lost to other schools in the county. Incidentally, the use of hutted classrooms is sometimes made the excuse for falling examination results. Yet in the case of Hazelwick the record year for exam successes co-incided with the peak of provision of hutted classrooms. If they were new, and the heating worked well, I preferred to teach in huts. One was insulated from distraction of disturbances in an adjacent class where a student teacher was learning to teach by 'breaking the class up into groups'. The main trouble with huts was the inability of contractors to erect them in the time promised. I learned to treat delivery dates with scepticism. The major building project, the new Upper School, was also not ready on time. I therefore had to draw up two plans for room allocations, one to cover the period of delay during which classes had to be held side by side in School halls, and one for use after the belated completion of Upper School. I often reflected on the general acceptance of failure to deliver on time in the world of business, and to make the unfavourable comparison with the inescapable obligation of schools to be ready to receive their pupils on the first day of term, even if, as was often the case, it meant the surrender of more than half the vacations, not to mention weekend after weekend during the Summer term.

The worst period for the timetabler is invariably the weeks after the 31st of May. Not until that date can it be known for certain which teachers who are seeking new posts will hand in their resignations. After that date their contracts prohibit resignation until the next term, so even if the timetable is well advanced before May, it is a lucky deputy who can get on with the really difficult final stages until June. After which, if he aims at really refined provision, he will have little time for gardening or weekend trips to the sea until late August. The fact that the staff at Hazelwick operated as a single team in Lower, Middle and Upper Schools meant that the road separating these buildings provided the final problem in the completion of the timetable. The last painstaking task was to read through all the fifty or more form timetables, and the ninety or more teachers' timetables to assess the amount of movement made by everyone between buildings and rooms. It took seven minutes for a class to move from Lower School huts to the top floor of Middle School. I therefore made final adjustments to eliminate such movements. The same applied to movements across the road. By reducing these to those necessitated by the siting of specialist rooms, and by breaking longer movements by placing a lesson in a half way room or hut, I contrived the elimination of hurried movement. I do not know which was the best timetable I ever made, but I remember the day in a September term when my wife was sitting with me in a room from which we viewed the spectacle of hundreds of boys and girls in royal blue uniforms, many in the pristine condition of newness. The movement of the children was ordered, relaxed and suggestive of maturity. My wife commented that it must be rewarding for me to see the proof of the painstaking care with which I revised the movement as shown on the timetable. Strangely enough I seemed to be the only person for whom this problem of movement was worth consideration. Ordered and unhurried movement ceased to be a feature of the timetable the day the Assistant Director for Secondary Schools arrived from Chichester with a jejune scheme for curricular areas. I pointed out to him the effect his scheme would have on the amount of movement, particularly across the road. He quickly took my point and made to withdraw his suggestion. But it was too late. The Headmaster's imagination had been stirred by the prospect of innovation. Nowadays the running from end to end of the campus at lesson change, the dashing pell mell between buildings, and all the shoving and short-cutting across the lawns can be seen by anyone who ventures along the road between the Schools.

In 1969 the total of O level subject passes topped seven hundred, excluding any passes which may have been gained at a second attempt. I do not know how this compares with other comprehensive schools with an uncreamed intake of about three hundred pupils a year. For me the satisfaction lay in the fact that it represented an increase of eleven hundred per cent in nine years. The number of grammar school pupils never amounted to more than approximately one form in each intake, for the New Town remained predominantly artisan in its social structure. The more representative English city would have provided a higher proportion of children whose parents had enjoyed grammar or public school education. For this reason I questioned the validity of comparisons with established grammar schools. My yardstick had to be the production chart of the School itself. Comparisons with other comprehensives in the New Town would have been interesting, but the information ceased to be available when our success became potentially embarrassing. The ever increasing demand for places at the School from parents living outside the catchment area, in some cases as far as the next town, seemed a fair indication of success.

When I compare the inordinate amount of time which I believed necessary to plan in complete detail both the timetable and the option schemes based on pupil preference and aptitude, with the dramatic improvement in academic results, I am convinced that the former was the direct cause of the latter. The one other factor which operated so favourably during these years was the steady improvement in the staff. I would find it difficult to know where to draw the line if I listed names. In my early days as Senior Academic Master I was rapped over the knuckles for telling a group of visiting students from a College of Education that, having regard to their meagre academic qualifications, they would be lucky to get a job at the School as I envisaged it. It was, I think the Principal of the College who phoned the Headmaster. In due course my indiscretion became accepted policy. Yet it was not merely a formula of good honours graduates for academic departments that obtained for the years of maximum success, the late sixties; the spread of exceptional talent in all departments reached a high tide. Then as, one after another, the best departed for headships or other promotion, the tide perceptibly ebbed. The change would not have been noticeable to a Governor or parent whose judgement was based solely on a list of staff and their qualifications. The adoption of a policy of internal promotions meant that vacancies in the total strength were made up by the appointment of probationer teachers, straight from College or University. The average age of the staff dropped year by year. At times I reflected ruefully that most of my colleagues were nearer in age to the prefects than to me.

There was no sign that the Governors were aware of these omens. My observation of Governors was limited to the few occasions when the Headmaster invited me to attend Governors' meetings, to be available to supply detailed information on academic issues. Typically I was never asked for any of the precise information which daily use had, as they say, placed at my finger tips. It was characteristic of all discussions to which I was privileged to listen that they gave force to the definition of the term 'discussion' which I most favour: the pooling of ignorance. I sat through a heated debate on the need for additional teaching rooms. Assertions were made. I was glad that no one, on that or any other occasion, asked me to verify them by reference to the charts of room-occupation with which I had equipped myself. I was spared embarrassment.

I also witnessed Governors at work on the all-important business of appointing staff. On rare occasions I took the place of the Headmaster, if more important business took him elsewhere. Some of the Governors were themselves graduates. This increased the measure and the confidence of their participation. They evinced, however, no greater awareness of professional considerations than their less educated colleagues. Indeed, it is in this vital matter of appointments that the amateurism of our system of schools is most evident. From my observation I learnt something of the irrelevant considerations that can gain or lose an appointment. The one I pass on to any ambitious young teacher applies only when the Governors are vocal, and not merely present to re-inforce the Headmaster. The mistake that is most likely to engender an antipathy in the Governors is the understandable desire of a good applicant to expatiate on the finer points of the teaching of his subject. The reaction of the Governors will not be one of appreciation. It is not agreeable to be lectured by an expert who leads his superiors out of their depth. The danger of being dismissed as a bore is very real. Answer the questions. Don't try and take over. If the questions include palpably fatuous suggestions on how to teach one's subject, conceal dismay and show respectful interest. If the interviewing panel is predominantly male and middle aged, then be a young woman with attractive features and a disarming smile. For such a candidate the acknowledgement of ignorance on any question will be far less damaging than the forceful asseverations of any experienced male applicant.

I must not go so far as to assert without reservation that the unusual number of attractive young women who worked on the staff was directly consequent upon this tendency. There were periods when the contingent of student teachers from Sussex University contained more than one whose attractiveness re-inforced that of the young ladies on the staff. This was never more apparent that on the occasion of a Parents' Evening in Lower School. The teachers were seated behind tables placed at intervals in rows along the hall. The Headmaster and myself were standing by the door to welcome and direct the parents as they arrived. One who was on terms of informal intimacy with the Headmaster came into the hall and surveyed the scene. He nudged the Headmaster with approval. 'You do know how to pick 'em, don't you,' he whispered.

It would, I think, surprise some parents to discover how competent at managing the more difficult classes some of these charming young women could be. Their resilience and self-confidence sometimes exceeds that of their male counterparts. This was particularly true of the exceedingly pretty young teacher who was roundly accused by a parent at one such meeting that she was obviously handicapped by reason of her age and attractiveness in the exercise of discipline. Her indignation at this patronising censure was fully justified. I often wished that some of the young men had possessed the same inner toughness of spirit. She and another attractive young woman shared a flat. One night they were woken by an intruder who escaped through a window in a suspicious state of undress. In due course the police arrived. For some time afterwards the police made friendly calls to see that the girls were all right. It was by nothing but co-incidence that the one who inspired such false misgiving in the parent should have left teaching after marrying a policeman.

I do not know how far the importance I attached to a very high level of sophistication in timetabling was one of the causes of my fatigue and withdrawal from teaching. As a Deputy Head and a teacher I had much else to attend to. I understand why in some comprehensives a teacher is allocated to nothing but timetabling. Yet it is not in the nature of things that such a situation should obtain. There are a number of circumstances which aggravate the problem of timetabling. They are far from inevitable. Much anxiety and delay was due to the insouciance of either Governors or County officials in setting up interviews. Whole weeks could elapse between the receiving of applications and the invitations for interview. The delay was often a reflection of the relatively low level of priority accorded to the making of appointments in the working diaries of Governors or County officials. The result for me was the bitterness of watching one good applicant after another withdraw the application in favour of a post elsewhere. On one occasion the procrastination was exceptionally galling. We had short listed six exceptionally good applications for a teacher of languages. The delay and unconcern was so protracted that everyone of those applicants withdrew, one after another. In the end the post was filled by a teacher who had a degree, but not in languages. Fortunately he had been long enough in France to qualify.

Two other circumstances that keep a teacher wholly or largely employed at the timetable are a high absentee rate on the staff, and a high turnover of staff. Both are regrettably more characteristic of large schools than small. In the course of one year a lady science teacher withdrew to have a child. The whole Science timetable was recast to cover the deficiency. After the birth the teacher returned to qualify for a salary entitlement. The timetable was readjusted. Then a second lady from the same department withdrew for the same reason, to return in due course. Finally the first lady resigned, having worked the qualifying period, or, perhaps because she found teaching and motherhood too much at the same time. Be that as it may, the Science timetable, involving a Department of nine teachers, was recast five times in one year. This sort of thing may have been unavoidable, but I never became reconciled to the indifference and exacerbation of the problem by a prodigal secondment of teachers on courses in term time. Every Christmas holiday I was back at work the day after Boxing Day, re-timetabling. I know well this to be so, because when I phoned County Hall for information about new or possible appointments, there was no one there.

I owe it to all those teachers, whether deputy heads or not, who find themselves grappling with the timetable of a large mixed comprehensive, especially those who are the victims of that ultimate folly of over-hasty enthusiasm for comprehensive schools at any price – I refer to the split-site school – to make a comment on the difficulty of timetabling. It is not merely the average parent with a reasonable grievance that there is no provision for an A level course, let us say, in Geology, Domestic Science and Latin, who finds it difficult to accept that there are limits to what can be written into a timetable so long as teaching for all classes can only take place between the immutable hours of nine to four. I was once given the chance to visit Waterloo Station and be introduced to the Assistant Stationmaster, who showed me, among other things, the station timetable for platform occupation. From the rapid calculations I was able to make, I estimated that the number of trains entering and departing from the Station each day was approximately the same as the number of lessons on the School timetable for each week. Making allowances for the fact that railways operate for the most part on timetables that remain the same for weekdays, it seemed to me that the School timetable presented greater difficulties. I noticed, for example, that one platform was occupied by a parcels train for most of the day. I reflected how much easier it would be if a class of children could be shunted into a room and left unattended for an indefinite period. Trains do not all have to move at the same time as do the classes in a school. And when they move they do not have to be broken up and then reformed into new combinations, such as are necessary to give effect to a complex system of school options. The comparison may be fanciful. All I can say is that Waterloo is a very big and busy terminus. I found little difficulty in reading the platform chart. No doubt I can never be fully aware of the imponderables that have to be written into its provisions. On the other hand I have known teachers at all levels who remain baffled by the complexities of the school timetable.

CHAPTER VIII

AN ORDERED WORLD: ONE'S OWN CHILDHOOD

I realise that when I attempt to discuss the question of discipline, and even more so the question of corporal punishment, I am entering a minefield of intense feelings. It will not do for me just to tell about my own experiences and to leave an impression of sitting on the fence, though, to be honest, I find that after reading the case for the abolition of corporal punishment in a book compiled by STOPP (Society of Teachers Opposed to Physical Punishment), I am less ready to leave the fence than I was before reading it. Indeed, such is the bewilderment that this and other books of that genre induce that I re-read them in search of the underlying but elusive premise on which these books are based. Why is it that the carefully tabulated accounts of who got caned for what, the pseudo-scientific data with which our sympathies are assailed, leave only the taste of dust and ashes. The quotations allegedly culled from the essays or conversations with children are equally perplexing. The impression of struggling and inadequate teachers, of bad schools, of a system in disarray is overwhelming. I recognise the teachers. The predicaments described are less familiar. It is the catalogue of the various forms of misbehaviour of children, some of them hardly out of the nursery, that give me the impression I am reading about a strange, alien world.

Like so many parents who have expressed surprise at what they learn about the character of contemporary schooling from their children, I inevitably look back to my own childhood, and wonder if my experiences of school were so exceptional. In short, the revelations of the abolitionists do not deepen my concern about punishments so much as they arouse disquiet and perturbation at the apparently commonplace nature of offences which one cannot imagine as possible in the secure and ordered world of one's own childhood. 'Walking out of the school without permission', 'throwing darts in class', 'tearing up books', 'smashing a bottle', 'throwing water about in the classroom', 'deliberately smashing a big window'. What on earth, I ask myself, is going on? Then a concern for truth compels me to remind myself that some of these offences have been committed in the comprehensive of which I was deputy head, but that, like the four thousand or more pupils who passed through the School during my time there, I never had the unhappy experience of witnessing any of these rare incidents, and am therefore in danger of being less than precise in my reaction to the emotive compilations on this matter of discipline. Yet the fact remains that to look back over one's own schooldays is to move into a happier world, untroubled by what seems to be the blight of present day schooling, the problem of defiant and disaffected children.

My memories of elementary school are vivid and clear. I must have been at elementary school from the age of seven to eleven, for I spent what seems like a year in each of five separate rooms. The men who taught us were, with one notable exception, all aged forty or more. I estimate that they must have been born in the eighteen eighties. Their minds would have been well formed in the decades before the Great War, as it used to be called. The exception was the youngest who had served as a soldier in the War. On reflection I can now recognise that his comparative youthfulness was matched by a difference in calibre. He was not quite in the same class as his colleagues. The teachers would assemble to chat briefly before school round one of the coal fires that were the only form of heating in the school. There was no staff room. The windows were high in the walls. Three of the classrooms were separated by movable screens. The desks and benches were long and heavy, firmly screwed to the floor by their metal frames. Such schools, so one is told, are still in use.

The strictness of the discipline of those days would, I suspect, surprise the young teachers of today, as would the fact that this strictness was never a cause of tension, let alone fear or unhappiness. It would not have occurred to any of the forty or so boys who packed those long benches, whose most essential equipment was a small tin containing a damp sponge with which to wipe clean the slates upon which we wrote, to question the fairness of the discipline. The use of the cane was frequent, usually one stroke on the hand. As far as I am aware, none of us regarded such use as a matter of any consequence, certainly not worth a mention to one's parents. There were, of course, no psychiatrists to discuss or stir up interest in school punishments.

Every teacher taught with a cane on his desk. It was used to quieten a talkative boy, or, as in my own case on one occasion, to punish the carelessness of ink on my fingers. Although my recollection is of a frequent use of the cane, I may be wrong. On the other hand the fact that those teachers, each closeted every day, all day, with the same forty boys, taught us so competently makes it more than likely that a reliance on the cane was unavoidable. I cannot imagine that a less summary method of correction would have resulted in anything but a lowering of standards and the erosion of the general contentment that prevailed. For I must stress that I cannot recall the cane being used repeatedly against any particular boy or as a manifestation of irascibility. Our acceptance of it reflected an unquestioning trust in the judgement of those most responsible of men, and if I had to choose between the schooling I received at their hands, with the one exception to which I shall refer, and the less happy days my own children spent in more modern junior schools, I can only say I am grateful that I went to school when I did. And here, surely, we must have come to the crux of the matter. For if I have no reservations about the fitness of men of such inflexible Victorian rectitude to teach with their canes visibly within reach, I am equally certain that I would be unhappy if some of the inadequate and unstable young men who featured in the school careers of my own children enjoyed a similar freedom of recourse to physical chastisement.

During my least year at this school I was taught in a large classroom into which were packed the two top classes in the School, each with its own teacher, the only separation between them being the gangway between the two centre tiers of desks. Such was the unquestioned authority of the two teachers that the attention of one class was not distracted by the activities of the other. Perhaps I do not do justice to these exceptional men in speaking of their 'authority', since this is a term which nowadays has pejorative overtones. Indeed, I suspect that it is a concept quite beyond the understanding of our present-day 'educationists' except as exemplified in the debased caricatures of their own tawdry stock in trade of jejune ideas. Authority is self-authenticating, and as such gives the freedom to teach without being incommoded by regulations that constitute a statement of mistrust and no confidence. The stern men who taught and taught and taught so relentlessly, without the diversions provided by the distractions of concerts, outings, sports days and the like, had the authority which gained unquestioning acceptance. It was characteristic of them that the announcement of names of those who had won scholarships to grammar school was followed by an instruction to the winners to stand and recite verses from the Venite, for this was a Church of England school. Whatever one may think of the appropriateness of such a procedure, it seemed to me at the time in no way remarkable, and, in retrospect infinitely preferable to the current practice of rewarding eleven-plus success with the gift of an expensive bicycle, or the iniquitous cajolery of parental interest which is withdrawn like the turning off of a tap in the event of failure. Perhaps the self doubt of so many young teachers today is the end result of this chronic obsession with academic failure that afflicted their parents. There was certainly no comparable distortion of relationships between adults, whether teachers or parents, and children, back in the nineteen twenties. It was by no means a perfect world in this matter of selection for the grammar school. The system was that set up by Balfour's Act of 1902. The grammar schools took only a quarter of their intake from 'free place' scholarship winners. The rest paid a small fee. This probably meant that more working-class boys gained places than under the Act of 1944, because the middle-class parents had no need to exert emotional pressure on the children to pass the eleven plus. The fee for those who by-passed the scholarship was absurdly small. Similarly there was a happy freedom from pre-occupation with O levels in the grammar school. The very existence of such a milestone in one's school career as the General School Certificate and Matriculation was not drawn to my attention until I had entered the fifth or examination year. Today GCE becomes a pre-occupation in many homes soon after the child has begun to learn to read.

I am not at all sure whether the more blessed features of my early school-days, the security and freedom from anxiety about the future, was typical. Of one thing I am much more certain: it would be difficult to find such advantages in the education-crazed world of today. There has been a dramatic increase in educational provision and expenditure. Education is an industry that rivals in its growth and peripheral ramifications that of the advertising industry. Yet the equally dramatic decline in the calibre of the average teacher, with the consequent rise of this post-war perturbation over discipline, suggests to me that advertising has been more successful in recruiting its labour force. Or are we to entertain the more depressing proposition that the decline in the intellectual and moral standards of our society is general, affecting all occupations and professions alike?

The playground of my elementary school was as bereft of amenity as were the classrooms; an asphalt area enclosed by a six-foot-high wooden fence. Neither the rigour of the classroom nor the smallness of the playground seemed to diminish our enjoyment of our unorganised play. Indeed, the fence was essential to our main recreation, a never-ending football match, played with a tennis ball, between the boys who lived in Beckenham and those who lived in Penge. It is seldom throughout our lives that we are vouchsafed those fleeting moments of felicity, for which the words enjoyment or pleasure are totally inadequate. One such moment, of unique and sweet fulfilment, rarely to be recaptured in the semi-conscious state of reverie and imminent sleep, but never by conscious mental effort, occurred on the day that the tennis ball rose, as if by magic and in a dream, to strike the fence in that part which by custom served as one of the goals. I am no enthusiast for football, having been introduced to the far more satisfying delights of rugby at the age of sixteen. The cult of soccer to which the vast majority of my fellow countrymen seem committed, particularly the violence to which it gives rise, is wholly repellent to me. Yet if I thought that it brought to either players or spectators moments of unalloyed bliss such as I experience from the goal I scored in that unrecorded contest with the tennis ball, I would regard the paroxysms of soccer crowds as justified. There was no room on that asphalt playground for such traditional games as 'jump-diddy-whacko'; the streets where we lived in the days before the scourge of the motor car gave us room enough for that. Cigarette cards, however, were used in a number of games where space was limited. One of the few occasions in my life when I succumbed to the temptation to cheat was in a game in which we competed for cards propped against the foot of a wall by flicking other cards at it and aiming to dislodge it. I had the idea that by sticking one cigarette card on to the face of another identical card I could enjoy the advantage of an unbeatable missile. The weight and thickness of my card did, in fact, prove unbeatable. I would like to think it was honesty that compelled me to reveal my duplicity, but I suspect it may have been a desire to show off my ingenuity.

For it is pertinent to my theme that I confess that I was a quiet, shy, and well-behaved child, what in briefer terms would be called 'a good boy'. This fact has more significance in view of what happened to me in my penultimate year at elementary school, when I was ten years old. The teacher for that year was the young ex-serviceman. The fact that he was not much older than thirty and was handsome made him the object of hero-worship. I did not escape this commonplace but childish infection, and wearied my parents with my infatuation with this immature young man. His dissimilarity from his older colleagues can be gauged from the fact that he succumbed to the temptation, common among teachers in the first or second year, to discuss his most personal experiences and pre-occupations in classroom digressions from the work in hand. I do not forget that I sinned in this way when I began teaching. It is an easy but ultimately destructive way to ingratiate oneself with audiences of captive children. From time to time the war-time reminiscences of our hero were re-inforced by our singing of 'Pack up your troubles' or 'It's a long way to Tipperary'. Our instruction in this accomplishment was always surreptitious and conducted sotto voce, revealing an obvious awareness of the possible reactions of teachers in the adjoining rooms. This sensitivity to unfavourable judgements from senior colleagues appears to me in retrospect a wholly favourable circumstance. Contemporary precepts in teacher training institutions has effectively weakened this inhibition on young teachers, who seem to regard the classroom as a substitute for the psychoanalyst's couch. This is so much so that I received, on one occasion, when I was deputy head, a bewildered comment from a parent that her child seemed to know more about what went on in the bed of his newly married teacher than the partner in these intimate experiences. It is possible that these confidences from an otherwise very able teacher were an attempt to give effect to that fatuous and meaningless exhortation to student-teachers to 'establish a relationship' with the children. Be that as it may, I am grateful that this particular precept had not yet gained currency when I was at school, and teachers proceeded on the more obvious assumption that a relationship is automatically established by placing an adult in front of a class, and that it is best to conduct proceedings on the assumption, accepted naturally by the children, that the teacher is paid to be there to teach. Our furtive renderings of war-time songs was my only experience of what has now become regrettably more common practice.

It was, however, in the course of a more orthodox singing lesson that a storm broke over my head. The class was singing from a large pendant chart on which was printed the diatonic scale in tonic sol-fa. In our attempts to follow the teacher's pointer by feebly singing the notes indicated we faltered incompetently. What followed must have been due to some sort of temporary loss of nerve by our teacher hero, a momentary touching upon some hidden point of sensitivity, of imagined inadequacy. It can happen to any teacher who has not learned from experience the extent of his own strength. As our singing faltered into silence I unthinkingly broke that silence by laughing at our contretemps. The teacher turned upon me in uncontrolled anger and subjected me to a tirade of abuse which seemed to have continued unabated for about a quarter of an hour. The only thing which I can remember from this torrent of denigration was the accusation that I was a 'little prig'. Perhaps this was true. The total effect of this passionate denunciation was to reduce me to tears. This was much more of a punishing experience than a judicial stroke with the cane. The teacher's anger, however, was unassuaged by this most uncharacteristic and lengthy tantrum. He ended by banishing me to a position of complete isolation, a place on one of the long empty desks at the back of the room. There was no reprieve for me from this ostracism, and I spent the rest of that school year in conspicuous isolation. I even thought it a sign of charitableness when, in the distribution of new pen nibs, I was approached by the teacher and received one from his hand, though no word was spoken on this or any other occasion.

The aspect of this sorry affair of which I am reminded when I read the intensely felt polemics of the opponents of corporal punishment is what appears to me the myopic unawareness or indifference of all parties to the vulnerability of children to uncontrolled and unrecorded verbal assault. I do not wish to suggest that a greater use of corporal punishment would serve better than wounding by verbal assault. I do, however, wish to voice a suspicion that a pre-occupation with the alleged evils of corporal punishment reflects a deep heresy of quasi-theological import concerning human nature, a sort of unspoken hint of the proposition that the human body is in some mystical way more sacred as a manifestation of human dignity than the human spirit. I hasten to refute any imputation that I hold to the view that corporal punishment is in any way more free from injustice than other forms of punishment. My father, who rarely spoke of his schooldays, was more than once moved to recall in unforgiving terms the occasion on which he was given one stroke with the cane for an offence of which he was innocent. He had drawn a line with a pencil with such care that his teacher accused him of having used a ruler. When he insisted that he had drawn the line freehand he was caned for lying. The impression made by this incident was such that he mentioned it more than once even late in life.

I felt no such indignation when I was so violently denounced and thrown out of my class at the age of ten. Perhaps this was due to the fact that I was too bewildered by the vehemence and general scope of the onslaught to recognise any specific offence, although I knew myself to be unjustly abused. Such was the intensity of my hero worship that I took perverse and masochistic satisfaction in a private avowal that the incident should not affect my adulation for my teacher. This may reveal something significant about me to a child psychologist, though whatever it was I soon grew out of it. As for the teacher, it will surprise no one who has had experience of the percipience of governing bodies to learn that he alone of that otherwise splendid staff was promoted to a headship. It is clear that a good profile wins esteem both in the classroom and outside it. A more weighty reflection stems from my attempts to compare the undeniable resilience of boys of my generation who played so happily under the restraint of a stern discipline with the querulousness of so many pupils where less certain notions prevail. Generalisations about different generations are difficult to sustain in the absence of rigorous research. Even if I could substantiate my suspicion about a decline in resilience, it would require exhaustive investigation into all manner of possible correlations, such as with formative influence or parents, changes in prevailing moral beliefs, and the changing status and attitudes of teachers.

Inflation of wages, particularly in occupations such as labouring, has eroded the respect formerly accorded to all sections of teachers. One can be confident of comparisons between past and present in considering this factor. I find it impossible to believe, for example, that a parent of a truanting child would have protested forty years ago against a mild punishment on the grounds that children should not be checked for doing what their parents so often do, namely to take a day off work when they feel like it. Such a protest was made in a letter to the Headmaster of Hazelwick. Similarly, the possession of a car is now so widespread among even the youngest teachers that boys and girls now go to school with little chance of constant encounters with their teachers, either as pedestrians, cyclists or passengers on public transport. This is a change the effects of which I believe to have been almost totally overlooked. At the school at which I worked from 1946 until 1956 there were for most of the time only two members of staff who possessed cars, one of whom was the Headmaster. A shortage of petrol might well be mitigated by a reduction in the number of people entitled to hold driving licences. To raise the lower age limit gradually year by year, making exception only of disabled persons and for vital purposes, until it became fixed at, say, twenty-five would not only relieve congestion in our cities and on our roads but it would have the salutary effect of bringing many more adults into contact with the juvenile part of our population. A greater awareness of realities may not always be agreeable, but it is invariably salutary. Headmasters and Headmistresses are legally entitled to exercise the same authority over pupils when they travel to and from school as when they are at school. The fact that the majority of teachers part company with pupils as they drive out of the school car park largely nullifies this area of supervision, often to the discomfiture of the pedestrian public.

Another aspect of school life which has changed radically since the War, and which is pertinent to standards of behaviour, is the expansion of the school meals service. When schools were smaller and most staff and pupils went home to lunch, a minimal provision had to be made only for a few sandwich eaters. It is during this interval between morning and afternoon school that the influence of the destructive minority in a school, of the unpleasant bully boys is at its greatest. On the one hand it cannot be stated too often that teachers are tired to a degree incompatible with maximum efficiency after four or five lessons. Their need of the lunchtime break is in some cases desperate. I tried to give recognition to this fact by asking the Heads of Schools to avoid allocating lunchtime duties to teachers unless they had a free period immediately before or after lunch. I have never heard of this provision being made anywhere else. On the other hand the need for supervision on a large unfenced campus is at its greatest in the lunch hour. The provision of a system of supervision by reliable and well-chosen prefects does much to alleviate the pressure on staff. Unfortunately the cult of egalitarianism manifests itself in multifarious and destructive ways. Prefects have been abolished at many schools, including Hazelwick, on the grounds that not everyone remains at school until eighteen. In an egalitarian society everyone should have the same chance of exercising prefectorial authority irrespective of age or character. By the same token presumably there is an unanswerable case for the abolition of the post of Headmaster, since only a small minority can enjoy the exercise of the responsibility of a headship, so long as appointments are confined to a selected few. The egalitarian argument becomes absurd when applied with logic to the full extent of its implications. Why, for example, should the post of Archbishop of Canterbury not be made attainable to more clerics, or of Prime Minster to more politicians?

Though few boys stayed at school during the lunch hour when I was at school, and while I think it feasible that children were less open to corruption when they went home for lunch, the hanging about in the playground was then, as now, the chief opportunity for the bully. I only stayed at school once when I was at elementary school. I cannot recall the cause, I remember very well, however, that as I was standing idly in the playground a boy very much bigger than myself came up to me and, without warning or explanation, struck me forcibly across the face. This was the first and last time I suffered in this way. I learn from my sons, however, that every playground has this hazard, more so when the school is large. For the non-combative child the exercise of wariness is a law of life on the lunchtime playground. I have read somewhere in the literature of the anti-caning zealots that the very existence of the cane in a school, even if it is not used, is analogous to the knowledge that there is a snake in the grass. I would be more impressed by this sort of advocacy if the same degree of concern and sensitivity were shown about the presence of the human menace to be found in every non-selective school and in a great many selective ones as well. The one who enjoyed striking me when I was a child is now a respectable shopkeeper.

Where then, it will be asked, do I stand on this question of corporal punishment in secondary schools? In the first place I dismiss as palpable sophistry the argument of Baroness Wootton, who justifies her campaign against corporal punishment on the ground that it is an anachronism in a society that has abandoned physical punishment for adults. If a man is detained in prison, even for one night in a police station cell, he is detained by physical force. The book compiled by the abolitionist teachers, the Society Opposed to Physical Punishment, is rightly published under the title A Last Resort. In the last resort a headteacher, whether or not he or she uses corporal punishment, has the right to pick up the phone and call on the physical support of the police when confronted with intransigent defiance. I have seen this happen. There is about the presentation of the abolitionist case more than a whiff of hypocrisy. My suspicion that underlying the whole campaign is a strong dynamic of escapism into fantasy is roused when I read at the end of the abolitionist book, A Last Resort, such passages as: 'For this book to end by suggesting a long list of possible alternatives to take the place of corporal punishment, would destroy its purpose, which is to indicate that the removal of corporal punishment, far from requiring the introduction of new forms of authoritarianism, paves the way for the development of creative relationships in which blind authority plays no part'. So there we have it. The real bogey is the existence in any shape or form of 'authority'. This inadvertent admission is followed by a feeble reference to an essay by a boy: 'You do not want to be afraid of someone, you would like to be friends.' It was this sort of contemptible escapism and sentimentality that led millions of otherwise sane adults to follow their leaders to the betrayal of Munich. I remember the then Archbishop of Canterbury welcoming the specious utterances of Hitler about his desire for peace. That doyen of High Church Anglicans among pre-war politicians, our Foreign Secretary, Lord Halifax, also had a strong propensity for friendship at any price, and exhibited no awareness of the incongruity of the spectacle of his joining the hunting parties of Herr Goering, the man who said that when he heard the word culture he reached for his revolver.

These exercises in the pursuit of 'creative relationships in which blind authority plays no part' can be very expensive. On the one hand we have the prototype in the pathetic national belief in the appeasement of Nazi barbarism. On the other hand we have in many of our secondary schools, at present afflicted with progressive headteachers or local authorities, the microscopic re-enactment of essays in appeasement. The greatest setback to the achievement of a steady rise in morale, behaviour and academic success which occurred during my time as deputy head at Hazelwick was the appointment as Head of Lower School of a disciple of Major W. M. Duane, of Rising Hill fame. For two or more years there was no corporal punishment in Lower School. My own office was in Upper School on the other side of the campus. For over five years I had enjoyed complete freedom from any anxiety about all aspects of life in Lower School, which was in the firm and conscientious hands of Mr G. W. Baker. The impact of the benign experiment encountering all disorder by well-intentioned chats included a sudden series of phone calls from teachers in Lower School, urgent requests to me to deal with hard and insensitive boys who were reducing young teachers to a mood of desperation by disrupting classes. When I pointed out that the Headmaster had ruled that matters of discipline were to be referred to the Head of Lower, Middle, or Upper School, as the case might be, I was answered by what I can only describe as a 'cri de coeur' that I would act in place of the Head of Lower School. The latter could not have stated his position more succinctly as when he said to me, 'Duane says that the presence or appearance of a Head Teacher among children should make no difference.' It is not for me to say whether or not Duane was being cited correctly. What disturbed me was that the Head of Lower School had achieved his aim only too well. His presence among pupils made less difference than that of the school caretaker. Meanwhile the deterioration in the level of civilised behaviour in Lower School continued, with a growing undercurrent of complaints not only from teachers but also from prefects. The latter were my direct responsibility and my appreciation of their voluntary unpaid concern for the School impelled me to appear in Lower School in that most heinous of roles, a figure of authority, much more frequently than for a long time. The Head of Lower School, a young man whose intelligence and high ideals I respected when exercised in any role but that of a schoolmaster, won promotion to a headship and for all I know may now be achieving success. His brief spell of Head of Lower School at Hazelwick did at least force me to face the dilemma which, if I have read between the lines of the Rising Hill story correctly, was one of Duane's problems. Do you respond or not to appeals for help in the form of punishment, from young teachers for whom there is no escape from immediate challenges from malevolent children?

Malevolent children. Is this not a contradiction in terms? Maladjusted children, deprived children, forgetful children, careless children, boisterous children, but surely not malevolent children? No indeed, if you accept the wholly deterministic assumptions of educational psychology. I realise that I shall have been very clever if I am not misunderstood. In all initial contacts with my fellow human beings I proceed on deterministic assumptions. I readily attribute any shortcomings, however disagreeable, to circumstances beyond their control. After all, I was reading Freudian psychology at the age of fifteen, and I was an enthusiast for A. S. Neill while I was still at school. Unfortunately I also suffered from an obsessional pre-occupation with the idea of free will. It is difficult for me to exaggerate my awareness as a young man of the centrality of this notion of free will. My mental exertions in my struggles to understand the implications of both free will and determinism, as I paced the banks of the Cherwell at Oxford, were far more strenuous than the physical exercise which accompanied my cogitations. Eventually I was told that my obsession was becoming a bore, and I forgot about it. It was not until I found myself as a deputy head constantly faced with urgent requests to administer punishments that I again began considering not only the validity of the concept of free will and personal responsibility, but its immediate relevance to the way I dealt with offenders. By this time the deterministic and environmental view of the behaviour of children or young persons at school had swept the board. I knew that if I proceeded to punish without waste of time or words those who were sent to me, I was consigning myself to the categories of the unenlightened, the 'squares'. This did not worry me, as my contempt for the intellectual calibre of all exponents of the psychological approach to teaching was inordinate. Not only did I find the utterances of those of the A. S. Neill persuasion shallow, as often as not devoid of any clearly stated premise, but my distaste for the sociological approach to behaviour problems was re-inforced by my attempts to dig down to whatever basic assumptions might make sense of the jejune ideas brought with them by the postgraduate students from the School of Education of Sussex University. I also soon lost patience with the practitioners at the Child Guidance Clinic, whose psychology was of the Freudian variety. Any discussion with them seemed based on the principle, 'heads we win, tails you lose'. If one suggested that a child should be exempt from the normal sanctions of school rules one was met with a vehement rejoinder that at all costs the child was to be treated exactly like all others. If on the other hand, one suggested that this might be the appropriate treatment, it evoked an equally emphatic rebuff. The subconscious motivation was paramount and precluded all routine procedure. Only one firm conclusion seemed to emerge from the abortive experiment of regular conference with the psychologists: whatever the line suggested by the Headmaster or myself, it was by definition the wrong one.

In practice, of course, my treatment of boys sent to me varied from the summary injunction to report to my office thirty minutes early each morning for a week, to prolonged endeavours to find a remedy for what seemed to be compulsive and repeated misbehaviour. The former treatment seemed appropriate and was usually effective in cases of infringement of simple and easily understood rules, such as the ban on running across the road. A more painstaking consideration seemed necessary when the same boy kept appearing outside my door on the charge of disrupting the lessons of young and inexperienced teachers. I remember one such boy whom I took around with me for a few days, as it was only by this means that I could find time to talk to him. When I had, as it were, broken down the reserves of our formal relationship, I asked him quite simply why he repeatedly disrupted the lessons of certain teachers. He replied with candour that 'he could not help it' with teachers who were not strict. It is perhaps one of the few advantages of a big school that I was able to deal with him by devising a timetable for him in which all his lessons were with strict teachers. Yet there are obvious limits to this sort of provision for special cases. It is worth commenting, however, that this boy's difficulty would not have occurred had the average age of the staff not been so uncommonly low.

I have met more than enough 'progressive' educationists to realise that in their view it is culpable negligence on the part of a teacher to be satisfied with this sort of remedy. It does not get to the root of the problem. It fails to uncover the cause of the child's disability. To which I reply that I can think of little that is more irresponsible and fraught with disastrous consequences than the role of amateur psychoanalyst. I am not sure that I would not extend my condemnation to some who are not amateurs. In the present state of knowledge available to us, it is not merely expedient but humane that we eschew the conceit of little knowledge and consider ourselves wise if we can remove the circumstance that stimulates difficult behaviours. The alcoholic must not be offered drinks. The headmaster who incites his staff to undertake the roles of an analyst or a social worker in addition to being a good teacher is a fool. The one offence for which a stroke with the cane was a punishment was smoking. In the first place the ban on smoking was complete and easily understood. In the second place the physical damage consequent on becoming a young addict could be far more horrific than any possible damage to the psyche of one stroke from a cane. Thirdly it was believed that all the evidence available to us indicated that by making smoking a hazardous way of challenging the authority of the School, we were keeping at one remove the more dangerous temptation to experiment with drugs.

Summary punishments of any kind imply the assumption that offenders are free to vary their behaviour, and that the punishment will encourage them to do so. May I take for example the matter of punctuality. When it became apparent that the marking of the register by form teachers was undertaken with differing degrees of accuracy, I deployed prefects to take names of boys or girls arriving late. The prefects were positioned so that a mere half dozen of them could see anyone arriving on the campus, even by way of the hedges on the far side of the playing field. Lateness was defined precisely to the minute. Latecomers had to report to me for a short detention on the same day, unless I was convinced that there were grounds for deferring it till next day. Now the point arising from this otherwise tedious narrative is that this certainty of detection reduced the incidence of lateness to one or two pupils a day in a school of sixteen to seventeen hundred. Sometimes, perhaps more often than not, the one or two latecomers had acceptable reasons which exonerated them. The same assumption and the same measure of success applied in the matter of homework. A series of surveys undertaken at my behest by postgraduate students gave a crudely scientific basis for a conclusion which could have been reached by surmise, namely that the amount of homework not done at home or not done at all, increased in inverse ratio to the ability of pupils. With this in mind I invariably set as homework for the less academic classes stints of work that would not tax their initiative overmuch. Writing up notes, drawing maps or charts, but rarely creative work which pre-supposed ideal home conditions and strong motivation for study. The boys also had the support of two certainties: I would ask to see the work done by each boy as he entered the classroom, and I would always mark it. Invariably I would also set simple tests on it of a degree of difficulty which made it possible for anyone who had done the homework to score between half to full marks. To set reading homework without testing it was, as my student surveys confirmed, tantamount to setting no homework.

Readers of these rather commonplace confessions may well be impatient for me to draw together the threads of my divagations into an affirmation of some sort of panacea. I find it easier to indicate pitfalls, to warn against plausible heresies than to reveal the text of an all redeeming formula. As an interim attempt to satisfy those who prefer their wisdom in nutshells, I recommend adherence to two maxims: don't expect a higher morality, a greater immunity from temptation in children than you are accustomed to find in adults; don't forget that the unforgivable sin against children who arrive at the classroom in fulfilment of a statutory obligation and not of their own volition is to waste their time.

The first of these admonitions implies the general readiness of most young people to comply most of the time with reasonable regulations. It also serves to remind one that a general compliance obscures a range of differences among any collection of individuals; this in turn causes some degree of tension when the ratio of pupils to teachers rises above family level. It is the desire to escape or to eliminate this tension, to pretend it does not exist that underlies most breakdowns of happy and fruitful relationships between teachers and taught. It is very difficult for some teachers, who cling to an idealised vision of children, to include in the range of their understanding the type of boy whose energy and toughness demands a regimen of comparable strength, an environment that does not yield to the strains they instinctively put on it.

An unusually robust but lazy boy whom I taught in a grammar school stated the predicament of the non-suggestible fearless boy for whom the normal moral pressures of a school are quite ineffective. I met him socially after he had left school. He told me, by way of an unsolicited comment on his experience of school that he was by nature lazy. The only one thing, he averred, that induced him to work at school was the Headmaster's cane across his backside. He was, in fact, the exceptional type who would have given a lot of trouble to the authorities in such institutions as Colditz.

It follows that, quite apart from the skills and knowledge which a teacher is paid to impart, the one thing essential for success in teaching in a non-selective school is judgement, the wisdom of insight and discrimination. It is rarely vouchsafed to the student teacher. On the other hand it is, I suspect, an innate characteristic which is developed with experience. It saddens me to state that it seemed totally lacking in many teachers. There are times when a sharp and immediate punishment is more appropriate than a judicial investigation. A boy guilty of obscene language to a young woman teacher may or may not have learned the habit at home. His re-education begins when he experiences the indignation of adults whose reactions are more representative of the society as a whole.

I remember being on the receiving end of the short sharp treatment when I was caught out as a boy, aged eight, in what must be a common enough peccadillo among schoolchildren, attempting to excuse failure to do homework by telling a lie. I had been absent from afternoon school. I had been to the dentist. I returned to school too late for lessons but not too late to play ball with a classmate on our asphalt playground. I cannot remember whether I asked about the homework, but I remember being told what it was. Next morning when asked to produce it I replied that I had not been at school when it was set. I was then discomfited by my erstwhile playmate who volunteered the information that he had told me the homework when I returned for a kick-about. The teacher's rebuke was succinct. 'I don't want a liar for a monitor.' I ceased to hold this much prized position forthwith. While I realise that this minor incident may well be regarded as reflecting little credit on any of us, I recount it because it impressed me profoundly. I had been judged a liar by a man whose authority I respected. I decided without hesitation that to tell lies for petty or for weighty considerations of self interest was a bad thing.

The recollection of this episode prompts reflection on its implications. It recalls to mind my life-long suspicion that the concept of free will is valid and that its consideration, its disinterment by those claiming an interest in moral education, is long overdue. The teacher whose rebuke impressed me so much that this trivial incident assumed the proportions of a formative experience, clearly assumed without reflection that I was responsible for what I said and did. What is more important it has hardly ever occurred to me from that day to this that, with the exception of one or two intractable weaknesses, to question the soundness of his assumption. I also reflect with gratitude that I did not, being at that time a suggestible child, fall into the hands of the sort of teachers who nowadays regards every misdemeanour an occasion, not for the exercise of that most essential and precious gift, a capacity for making a judgement, but for a benign investigation into motivation. I am not against such investigations and I confess that I have spent much time investigating not merely culpability but also motivation. Yet I hold strongly to the view, one which is fervently endorsed by the majority of well-adjusted children, that it is an insult to any man, woman or child not to pay them the common courtesy of an a priori assumption that they do what they do of their own free choice. Not until indications emerge of circumstances to justify it should we arrogate to ourselves the dangerous and patronising role of the omniscient psychoanalyst.

Bertrand Russell was not, when it came to the matter of morals, unwise to pretend that human understanding can answer all our demands for reductionist explanations. Cruelty is wrong. Kindness is preferable to cruelty. These are propositions that command acceptance but defy proof. Thus we are back again at the idea of moral authority, self-authenticating, and as such, totally compelling. It will be one of the tasks of future historians of education to seek an explanation of the rapid declension of educational theory into the slough of sentimentality and muddleheadedness that has characterised it during the past two decades. From the impressions I have gained from talking to some of the more intelligent and non-suggestible youngsters who have repudiated the assumptions currently regarded as progressive by contemporary pundits, there will eventually be a return to reality. In the meantime we must expect many of the most responsible posts in our large prestigious comprehensives to be thrown away on those for whom 'authority' is a dirty word and whose intellectual equipment is not equal to grappling with the full implications of the concept of responsibility. It was with dismay bordering on despair that I watched a TV interview with a newly appointed headmaster of a famous London comprehensive. He was asked what his reaction would be to the deliberate smashing of school windows. With predictable fatuity he replied that he would be less interested in culpability than motivation. I confess that I would share an interest in a compulsive window-breaker. Yet it escapes and defeats my comprehension that any normal man should have difficulty in understanding the impulse to throw a brick through a window. I used to experience an almost irresistible desire to do so every time I passed a particular shop that inflicted a deafening blast of pop music on innocent passers by. If I had known that the consequence of a lack of restraint on my part would be no more painful than a discussion of my motives I would have found the temptation irresistible.

Temptation. Another discarded concept. It is an inseparable part of the mental furniture of the anti-authoritarians that they invariably attribute, by implication, a far more developed sense of responsibility and moral awareness to the young and the immature than to fully grown adults. It is thus not regarded as a mark of depravity among adults that the temptation to break speed limits should be mitigated by the visible presence of police cars. On the other hand I have had to listen to two of Her Majesty's Inspectors seriously suggesting that teachers were not really needed in a classroom after work had been set. They were not talking about sixth formers or top-stream academics. Low-ability classes, provided the work was carefully chosen and 'geared' to the interest and ability of the class, had no need of supervision. These men must have been teachers at one time. How long does it take a teacher who has escaped the daily confrontation with reality to develop this occupational disease of thinking in terms of fantasies about idealised children.

Having become accustomed to taking charge of morning assemblies, I retained in the most lively part of my consciousness the daily call to Almighty God to 'lead us not into temptation'. For this reason I developed a constant awareness of the sort of temptation which would inevitably arise from compulsory attendance by children at approximately fourteen hundred lessons a year. I noted their instinctive and often successful efforts to mitigate the tension of their situation by turning it into a social event by grouping themselves in a way that made talking to their friends more easy. I noticed also that this made sustained interest more difficult. I reminded myself that BBC talks were planned on the assumption that interest and attention of voluntary adult listeners could not be held for more than ten to fifteen minutes. With such considerations in mind, I made it difficult for pupils to attend to anyone but me. With the experience of a stable syllabus I learned to know what excited interest without resorting to digression. Some form of activity, other than listening to teacher, had to form the major part of every lesson. Repetition with differing presentation was popular and rewarding. Finally the achievement of mastery at work, even at the price of some drudgery, proved a far more powerful incentive than the constant pursuit of ephemeral interest.

All of this is of course the familiar stock-in-trade of the successful teacher, though not of those who immolate themselves by breaking the class up into groups and launching themselves into the quicksands of projects. My reason for drawing attention to it is to promote a more constant consideration of ways in which the idea of temptation, about which we pray, albeit perfunctorily, may be applied to the classroom. There remains for me one unanswered question. If it were to happen, as is most unlikely, that a child were to be taught by none but stimulating, successful, and demanding teachers, what is the optimum amount of such teaching that the average child could stand? Does every class have to find a weak link in the chain? Is it conceivable that there has to be at least one teacher on the timetable of every class whose lessons achieve little apart from a letting off of steam?

The situation is hypothetical. The classroom situation in non-selective schools is stark in its simplicity. The modes of behaviour governing other situations in which teachers meet children do not apply. It is a unique situation with its own psychology. There have been of late many attempts to observe classroom behaviour scientifically. The accounts of such attempts of which I have read have been vitiated by a disregard of imponderables, such as the vast range of teaching ability as well as learning ability. There is also a tacit disregard of the coercive basis underlying compulsory schooling. A permissive technique is too often an attempt to escape the tension of the fact that the children are there because they have got to be there. I am convinced that it is helpful for a teacher to think of the psychology of the classroom not only as unique but also as analogous to a sexual confrontation. In the first place a child will behave quite differently when asked home to have tea with a teacher. Different rules will apply. Yet it is an illusion to think that these rules will automatically be carried back to the classroom. A group of children compulsorily assembled is like a woman lured into the receptive position that precedes seduction. She will not take kindly to the situation if nothing happens, or if the initiative is suddenly passed to her. The same, of course, applies to any group of adults who have been assembled in front of a platform. They will expect to be assailed by something more than an invitation to make themselves comfortable. In this sense the teacher adopts a masculine role, even if it is a woman teaching boys. But this is no cause for demur. The most hardened soldiery quickly adopted the psychological posture of expectant virgins when assembled to be addressed by a forceful commander, like Montgomery.

I have been looking at my punishment books for my last five years as a deputy headmaster. It confirms my impression that the School was in its hey-day from about 1966 to 1970. In January 1967 I caned one boy for starting a fight in a Maths class. The next was not till March. The Summer term of 1967 seems to have been without incident. Three canings for separate incidents are recorded at the beginning of December. The Easter term in 1968 produced two canings, one of which I remember well. An elderly gentleman arrived at the School indignant and agitated because a boy had insolently knocked his hat from his head as he passed him on a cross-country run. He had no difficulty in identifying the culprit, and was understandably resolved to see that the boy did not escape with a mere lecture on manners. In the Summer term of 1968 I caned a boy for attempting to escape from a detention by climbing out of a window. Three fifth formers attempted to cut classes after the exams and truant to the Youth Wing for table tennis. In the September term there would have been no entry had I not come upon a riotous incident in an Art room. The first term of 1969 added one entry to the record. The Summer term produced two entries.

The incidence of these canings, or assaults upon children as the Secretary of the Council for Civil Liberties preferred to call them, must be judged against the fact that it was at the time when the School was at its peak both in numbers, about seventeen hundred, and in its achievement in exam successes. It was in 1969 that the number of O level subject passes exceeded seven hundred. In my last complete academic year the number of entries in my book increased to nineteen for the year. This could be attributed to the unusual number of outstanding teachers who had been promoted to other schools, but I suspect that it reflected my own disabling tiredness. In January 1971 I posted my resignation to County Hall. Somewhere along the line it had been suppressed, for I was told, quite incorrectly, that I had asked to withdraw it. A year later I asked for a sabbatical year in which to recuperate from exhaustion.

This request was unanswered. In the meantime I had handed my resignation, in person, to the local Education Officer.

I hope that the staffing of our schools will one day become the over-riding priority for those who determine these matters. Looking at the names of those who bent over in my study I see none whose sensitivity was such that it could have been a traumatic experience. Yet I concede that had the average age of the staff, and the thirty or so student teachers whom we accommodated, been ten years nearer the average for the country, and had I enjoyed more time for dealing with miscreants, we might have anticipated the benefits of higher staffing standards, among which may be included the abolition of corporal punishment.

It remains to be recorded that a stroke from the cane was far from being regarded as either the most severe or effective punishment that was available to us. In the case of a compulsive disrupter of lessons whose activities reflected an inordinate desire to play to the gallery, the most sure remedy was a transfer to a class in the next age group, preferably of an ability which enabled the offender to continue working. Boisterous bully boys have no standing among their seniors, and their discomfiture becomes apparent in their hang-dog looks within a week or two of their promotion. Yet there remains the consideration of the question I posed in rhetorical form, but which for many wretched teachers is far from rhetorical. Can we with justice refer to 'malevolent' children? There was one incident in which the malefactor was a large, strong and brutal boy who had come to us for the last few months of his school career. I cannot be sure that he would have been a more agreeable person had he come earlier. His family included criminals. His prowess at intimidation was first brought to my notice when I discussed with his class the pros and cons of form prefects. When they expressed interest in the idea I asked them if they could think of a suitable nominee. The answer was a unanimous acclaim, the menacing character from London. I asked the reason for their preference. 'He can knock down anyone who argues with him.'

On the last day at school, during the break, when all the staff were gathered for end-of-term farewell formalities, the proceedings were suddenly interrupted by the repeated ringing of the fire alarms. As a result of prompt action the bully of the Fourths and a less impressive admirer of his were caught running down the stairs from the broken fire alarm. Three sixth-form girls boldly attested to the fact that the boys had descended the stairs shouting 'I've done it. I've done it.' This was not conclusive proof of guilt. There were, however, two girls who had seen the deed. And here I come to the point of the story. Their terror of the culprit was so immediate and overwhelming that they wept for fear when the senior mistress asked them to identify the two boys. Not only did they refuse to speak but asked to be seen safely home. Confronted by the Headmaster and the sixth-form girls who witnessed their precipitate descent of the stairs, the two boys were quite unabashed and left the School loudly proclaiming their moment of triumph: 'You didn't see us, you didn't see us.'

At one point in his masterpiece, his Autobiography, that giant among the writers of the early twentieth century, John Cowper Powys, digresses from his inimitable narrative to speculate on human experience. He surmises that the most significant aspect of the cosmic drama is an unending conflict between the forces of good and evil. I will not attempt to reduce this observation to the terms of any contemporary and fashionable branch of knowledge. I am content to say that I think it is true.

CHAPTER IX

DREAM AND REALITY

Fantastia, states my dictionary, is a pre-occupation with thoughts associated with unobtainable desires. As such it must stand high in any list of the occupational hazards of teaching in secondary schools, the more so in comprehensive schools where the pressures on teachers to immolate themselves in the pursuit of the unobtainable bear heavily upon them from above. To the visions of high-minded head teachers, who owe their promotion as much to the plausibility of their sentiments as to the loftiness of their aspirations, must be added the less innocent axe-grinding of Chief Education Officers who operate with at least one eye on the weather vane of political events, the changing composition of Education Committee and the policy-makers at Curzon Street. Yet even in the undisturbed backwaters of the most inward-looking grammar school the gap between the most dearly cherished dream of the individual teacher and the reality of what actually goes on in the mind of a boy or girl is the source of most palpable stress. I have a clear recollection of an informal gathering of teachers after a staff meeting at Ifield Grammar School, as it then was. It was a fine September evening. Some of us had just adjourned to the pub opposite the School after the annual staff meeting on the day before the School re-opened for another academic year. There had occurred nothing untoward at the meeting, which had been conducted by the Headmaster with commendable efficiency and briskness. As for the coming re-organisation which was to destroy the School, it was not yet the proverbial cloud on the horizon, no bigger than a man's hand. The circumstances seemed favourable to the convivial re-union of colleagues and friends, returning refreshed by the long summer vacation. Yet so sombre was the mood of that forgathering that I made a comment on what seemed to me to be a tenseness of anticipation, a tautening of the mind against the coming strain of another year. All of those present confessed that this was so. A momentary awareness of the fragility of our refurbished visions of bright new classes responding to secret resolves must have passed between us.

Fortunately the element of fantasy in a teacher's thinking about this work is well nigh indestructible, so long as the organisation supports him with an ordered routine, a predictable sequence of manageable encounters with tractable and tolerant children who have learned to accept if not enjoy the idiosyncrasies of those set in authority over them. It was a teacher of music at this same grammar school who had so far achieved a measure of self knowledge as to remark with wry humour that he learned to counteract the mental excitement of every fresh idea for improving his teaching by the discipline of imagining its operation on the mind of an actual pupil, more precisely a pupil of unassailable indolence, non-suggestibility and indifference. Much good might well be achieved for the children of this country if lecturers in teacher-training institutions, as well as these who write books on teaching, were to subject themselves to this very simple exercise in intellectual integrity as a daily routine. Better still, if a generation of teachers were to emerge in whom the need for the constant resort to introspection in search of reality was deeply instilled, some of the hopes of those who legislate in these matters might find fulfilment. This is, of course, as unlikely a development as is the larger objective of a universally successful system of comprehensive schools providing the highest and all-transforming education, without exception of limitation, to every child in the land. Even if the run-of-the-mill teacher could transcend all limitations of intellect, of innate temperament, of nervous resources, the unpalatable fact would remain that it takes many years to reach maturity as a teacher. I confess that I derive little satisfaction from the recollection of my first fifteen years as a schoolmaster. Making every allowance for my congenital perfectionism, and writing off, as it were, the excusable blunders attributable to both the callowness of my first two years and to the exhaustion of my last two years, I remain sobered by even the most flattering computation of what I may have achieved in the many thousands of my classroom appearances.

It was always a matter of regret to me, during my twelve years of intimate and daily communication with my headmaster, as we strove to the limits of our respective strengths to give effect to our vision of what a comprehensive school ought to be, that I did not share his capacity for making the School an arena for the celebration of the very fact that it existed, and more particularly, that he was indubitably the Headmaster of it. My nagging pre-occupation with the productivity of teaching, of sustaining an uninterrupted day-by-day impact on each and every child of approximately fourteen hundred lessons a year, sometimes conflicted with the more congenial occasions on which the achievements of the School, whether academic or in any other of the traditional category, could be publicly proclaimed or advertised. His exasperation with me when he berated me for 'thinking of nothing but teaching' was understandable. The contrast between his generous tolerance which characterised his relationships as a man among men and the impenetrable irrationality of his mental processes when he succumbed to the full force of fantasia on his view of himself as the headmaster of the best of all possible schools amounted to a paradox. It was a circumstance that alone explained the discrepancy between the impression he made on those who encountered him in his role as the spokesman for the School, such as the numberless batches of visitors to the School, and on those of us for whom the realities of any particular situation were matters pertinent to practical and urgent problems. To draw attention to considerations which disfigured the official and immaculate image of the School was a delicate operation calling for tact and timing. Even so, reality had a way of breaking through, and bringing in its train the hazards of uninhibited castigation. There were, of course, other members of staff in whom an extreme extroversion could be the cause of irascible outbursts, but the freedom of manoeuvre afforded to me by my position as deputy head in dealing with them made them more tolerable.

It is possible that a reflective introvert such as myself, one to whom all human utterances appeared at first to warrant the consideration of considered statements, of consistent and irreversible attitudes, was not the ideal choice for deputy head to an impresario manqué. Be that as it may I was sufficiently conscious of my Headmaster's redeeming virtue in his professional role as to wish to place it unambiguously on record. To castigate his assistants, sometimes with an impulsiveness that seemed to preclude any possibility of judiciousness, was a privilege not to be shared by anyone else. I can only recall one instance when mounting parental pressure of criticism of a teacher reached County Hall and evoked extra-mural intervention. Otherwise the energy and realism of the Headmaster provided an umbrella of protection and advocacy the extent of which was not fully appreciated by rank and file members of staff. There were other headmasters working for the same Authority whose idealism gained the appearance of rationality from their greater equability. The weakness of such passionless virtue would, I suspect, have been all too apparent to the wretched young teacher who, having been provoked to transgress beyond the limits of the professional code, stood in desperate need of support from his headmaster.

The higher one stands in the hierarchy of a school the more difficult it becomes to remain detached and objective in one's attitude towards it. I confess to a mild loyalty to those schools in which I was one among many, but I well remember that my standing among the sixth formers at one school was immediately boosted by their discovery that I was not noticeably infected with what used to be known as 'school spirit'. Setting aside the perennial taste of sixth formers for iconoclasm, it should surprise no one that young teachers maintain cooler attitudes to their schools than older ones. So long as aspirations after promotion endure, the first two or three jobs are regarded as but temporary sojourns in an onward and upward progress. To which consideration must be added the overriding emotional involvement, for me at any rate a paramount one, in the adventure of marriage and the bringing up of children. Indeed, the importance I attached to the latter was such that I disregarded entirely the salient rule for teachers who are hell-bent on becoming headmasters, the need to accept, if need be, the expense and inconvenience of repeated house moves. It ill accorded with the conceit with which I regarded myself that I should have turned down jobs in other schools after successful interviews and remained in the same post for the whole of my thirties, particularly after having spent six years of the previous decade not in teaching but in the Army. This self-imposed immobility during, if only I had known it, the years of maximum resilience and energy was due solely to my refusal to diminish the amenities which I considered proper for my children's enjoyment. The diary which I sporadically wrote during those years highlights the order of my priorities, intermingling soul-searching speculations about the value of my work as a teacher with entries about long excursions with my children into the country on some of which at least one of them was in a pram. In this matter I regret nothing. The adult company of my children is my reward.

At an age at which my chances of changing schools might have been regarded as perilously near to becoming negligible I decided to apply for a post in a new town in Sussex. My motive was still typically my desire to find a home for my family in countryside further from London. The comparative freedom of rural areas, even in the Home Counties, from saturation by motor cars was still at that time such as to enable one to think in these terms. A job in the New Town carried with it the option of a rented house, a base from which to search for the ultimate domicile. My subsequent appointment to the post of the senior factotum in a new comprehensive was thus an unforeseen and fortuitous culmination to a teaching career characterised by a sluggish and irresolute response to the spur of ambition. At the age of forty-five, a few weeks before I was so fatefully inveigled into my all-absorbing involvement in comprehensive schooling, I confided to my old wartime friend Keith Sewell, whom I had met at a conference of Assistant Masters, that I was thinking of settling for the job I had got. Like so many teachers of my generation I had not reckoned with the violent disturbance which 're-organisation' was to inflict, like deep furrows ploughed askew across a well-developed garden, on the careers and plans of so many of us.

There was never any chance of my coming to regard Hazelwick Comprehensive School, despite its spell of success and acclaim, with the sort of uncritical affection evoked by older and more prestigious selective schools. The presence in a comprehensive of a sizeable contingent of pupils for whom one school is much the same as another is a circumstance that constantly inhibits the development of any cosy inward-looking complacency. For such pupils the spread of 'school spirit' is a non-starter. Those who belonged to the rugger or netball or swimming teams, or who enjoyed the applause at play productions, might well become imbued with a sense of the peculiar superiority of their school. The proportion of the school, however, who were untouched by such activities and occasions, was too considerable not to diminish the degree to which teachers, accustomed to the more wholesale involvement of pupils in more homogeneous schools, could identify themselves with the fortunes of the place of their employment.

On the other hand the extent to which the work and organisation of the School came to reflect my distilled ideas, the fruit of years of cogitation, made my feelings about the success or failure of Hazelwick too intense for the luxury and palliative of rose-coloured spectacles. You cannot, as it were, be present at a Battle of the Somme and imagine a state of affairs markedly different from that which actually obtains. Every lesson badly taught, every trivial misdemeanour, every manifestation of oafish unruliness, both in school and out of it, every word on a lavatory wall registered in my mind as a casualty. Two years after my withdrawal from the engagement I could still not see a group of schoolboys in a street, irrespective of school or town, and not wonder whether their behaviour and intentions were all that they should be. I was like Robert Graves, who in his 'Goodbye To All That' tells how, after his demobilisation, the sight of a farmhouse set him calculating how best to attack it. My successor as deputy head, a younger man than me on his way up, was capable of detachment, and it did not surprise me that he gained promotion after a short stay at the School.

This whole question of what is right and proper for both teachers and pupils in the matter of feelings about one's school has not, as far as I am aware, been adequately investigated and discussed. It may be that it is not possible to investigate it, except superficially. Some children can be as secretive and pokerfaced as to their innermost feelings about the tribulations unwittingly inflicted on them by well-meaning adults as some husbands about their wives, or wives about their husbands. What I deplore is the confidence of Speech Day utterances in which the sentiment that all is for the best in the best of all possible worlds is expressed with such plausibility as to overwhelm the critical capacity of an entire audience. Equally reprehensible is the assumption by some teachers, more particularly by those who have strongly identified themselves with their schools, that there is something culpable in the attitude of youngsters who, for reasons which they might find difficult to articulate, do not entertain feelings of unalloyed affection and loyalty to the school to which fate has allocated them. Underlying such an assumption is the questionable premise that benevolence of intention is the equivalent of benefits conferred, and that in recognition of this there is a moral obligation on every member of a school to regard it with unalloyed feelings of gratitude and loyalty.

In the case of my own experience as a boy at a pre-war grammar school there was no need for the Headmaster or any of his assistants to concern themselves about fostering a school spirit; no need to insist on the School uniform to mitigate tensions of heterogeneity of social backgrounds. I cannot recall a single instance of a boy expressing dissatisfaction or voicing a criticism of the regimen to which we so readily conformed. The teachers suffered no harassment in the classroom, and in the greater part of the multifarious out-of-class activities their role was barely supervisory. The competitions between the six Houses were organised and refereed by sixth formers. Contests in dramatic and musical activities flourished under the management of House prefects. The staff were able to reserve their energies for major School events. Among the more important athletic events was an annual contest against the grammar school about which Malcolm Muggeridge has written with so little enthusiasm. The support of both schools on these occasions was large and vociferous, with the victors being carried on shoulders to the presentation of the cup. Those whose experience of schools has been confined to the post-1944 epoch cannot imagine the exhilaration of life at a good pre-war grammar school. For me the epitome of these excitements was provided by my friend and sometime mentor in matters non-academic, a tall athletic boy, Norman Piper. He invariably excelled in the quarter mile. Before participating in an athletics match he would establish the mood by playing a record of that racy piece by Sousa, The Stars and Stripes.

Running in the School cross-country team was in my case the least of my involvements. Incidentally we used the course of the Blackheath Harriers, now much diminished by the spread of suburbs. I played rugger and hockey, acted in plays, sang in choirs, played in the orchestra and military band, spoke in debates, contributed to the School magazine, refereed in House matches, all the usual things in which all boys seemed so ready to participate and co-operate with an enthusiasm undebilitated by such post-war distractions as television or part-time employment. The School did not absorb absolutely all our energies. We were near enough to London to go to Promenade concerts or to opera at the Old Vic or Sadlers Wells. Not being a cricket player I was free to go camping at summer weekends in a countryside undisturbed by motor cars, where in the privacy of an isolated tent we were able to enjoy interminable colloquies on that most pressing of all problems, in which our School was of no help at all, how to make contact with the opposite sex.

I had not long returned to schoolmastering after the War before I realised that my own schooldays provided no reference upon which to base judgements about the schools in which I worked. Not only did the arrangements of R. A. Butler's Education Act produce less homogeneous communities in secondary schools than the part fee-paying part free-place grammar schools which they superseded, but the social and economic changes which followed the war, particularly the opportunities for young people to earn money, steadily weakened the formative influence of schools on their pupils. In any case I have never been able to make up my mind whether the seeming richness of my days in the sixth form was absolutely and without qualification a good thing. The thought that this might not be so first occurred to me when, just before my nineteenth birthday, I had to make the wrench and finally leave school. Such was my infatuation with the place that it had become for me the centre of the universe and my feeling for it amounted to a fixation which was no help in growing towards a maturity.

When I say that I finally left school I have in mind the fact that I had already left school once before. By the time I had matriculated through the General Schools Certificate exam the economic depression was at its worst. An inarticulate concern for the financial circumstances of my parents made me accept without consideration the chance of diminishing their burdens by entering upon an apprenticeship in pharmacy in a chemist's shop in Pimlico. Perhaps if I had foreseen the fortunes which were to be made in subsequent years by successful pharmacists I might have persevered in Pimlico. But those were the times when shopkeepers were committing suicide. I remember being surprised and mildly shocked at the obsequious deference shown by the otherwise taciturn pharmacist to any of his customers whose appearance suggested an income noticeably above the average. Yet it was no such consideration that led me to eschew the pestle and crucible. My return to school was due solely to the perception and compassion of my father who must have observed in my aspect the settled mood of abnegation in which I made my daily journey to Pimlico. I hope he had some inkling of the unexpected felicity I experienced when without warning he suddenly asked me whether I would like to go back to school. I had no idea that such things were possible. My father, it seems, had already discussed the matter with the Headmaster, who in turn made an application for this incredible reversal in my fortunes at the County Education Office. I surmise that the Headmaster was influenced in my favour by the belief, in which he was later justified, that I might do credit to the School by winning an open scholarship to Oxford. Sidney Gammon had only recently been appointed Headmaster at Beckenham. I was the first of the many boys who won Oxbridge awards from what had previously been a school of no academic distinction. Sidney Gammon, who as a young man had survived the Battle of the Somme, in which he was wounded, was killed in the next war by a bomb dropped on his home in an air raid. The success he initiated for the School in the Oxbridge stakes continued for some years under the next headmaster. I was sorry to learn that in the end the School as I knew it disappeared in the spate of re-organisations of the last decade.

I find it hard to believe that the uncritical enthusiasm with which I embraced the opportunities for the enjoyment of life when I returned to school as a sixth former was really a bad thing. My son, the one whom I transferred to Hazelwick during the brief period of its success, probably enjoyed his days as a sixth former as much as I did, with the additional advantage of friendships with girls and the complete absence of that slight whiff of pederasty which underlay the enthusiasms of some sixth formers in a pre-war boys' grammar school. My daughter and my elder son remained sadly untouched by any feelings for their respective schools, the former being still unable to enter a school without immediately reacting with an attack of uncontrollable yawning. The latter refused to stay at his comprehensive school long enough to sample the benefits of the sixth form, and this despite or perhaps because of the fact that he is the acknowledged 'brain' of the family.

Even if I have to concede that the excellence of all aspects of life in a pre-war grammar school as experienced by me has now become impossible in the world of child-centred education and demoralised teachers, I suspect that the memory of high standards has been the most potent factor in making me and others of my generation the least complacent of teachers. I think, for example, of the enjoyment of being taught by a music teacher like Hubert Clifford. Before coming to this country he had been conductor of the Melbourne Symphony Orchestra. His demands upon those of us who joined the School orchestra were exacting and intransigent. Rehearsals began on the stroke of four fifteen each Thursday when he strode into the Hall and without any ado raised his baton like the professional he was. There was no question of our not being ready, of belated setting up of music stands or giving out music, of tuning our instruments. There were times when he seemed to us as some sort of slave driver. We inwardly cursed the day we became involved in his enterprises. Then we would go to the Queen's Hall in London and carry off the first prize in the national contest for school orchestras. Our satisfaction in the knowledge of our superiority resulted in the continuation of weekly rehearsals throughout the school holidays, at our request. These achievements and satisfactions owed nothing to child-centred teaching.

The deep-seated preference to belong to institutions or groups which demonstrate a superiority in performance and attainment reminds me of a comment made by John Strachey in his 'End of Empire' about the readiness of the Indians to fight for the East India Company in the subjugation of their own countrymen. It was, it seems, an example of this readiness to accord loyalty to an efficient and demanding organisation, albeit an alien one. The craze for egalitarianism which is currently corroding the efficiency of our schools takes no account of the great stimulus to human endeavour that this loyalty to 'a good show' provides. During the war against Hitler there was some research into the problem of how to achieve a good fighting morale. I remember reading about it in one of those slender pamphlets which were distributed to junior officers who were supposed to instruct troops-in-training about 'Current Affairs'. A high morale, it seems, was not a response to the enunciation of great principles of universal validity, like freedom or democracy but was a reflection of strong sentiments about what was proper for a member of a group much smaller and more easily identified than humanity in general, such as the family, or one's town or county. The same conclusion could have been reached by reference to the literature of the First World War, which testified abundantly to the power of loyalty to one's comrades in a regiment or battalion. A larger loyalty can only derive from the strength of smaller ones. A strong predilection for the welfare of 'the people' or 'the masses' as evinced by militant or doctrinaire progressives comes more easily to those who are unencumbered by a concern for smaller and more identifiable groups. The parent whose lefty principles cause a child to be sent to a bad state school so that principles shall not be compromised is to me a far less attractive person than the socialist whose desire to do the best for his children is incompatible with toeing the party line.

Looking back on my days in the sixth form I try to account for the totally agreeable quality of that phase of my life. Perhaps it would have seemed less exhilarating if my father's income been large enough to provide more diversions at home; if, for example, he had been able to afford to entertain visitors at home in the manner of middle-class families. I doubt it. My subsequent experience of more affluent social circles has seldom resulted in the widening of my cultural horizons on a scale comparable to that which followed my return to school. I find it difficult to recollect any other setting in which so much encouragement was given to the full unhindered expression of my personality without my encountering some abrasive and frustrating element in my environment. The world of school was the microcosm of the world as it should be. Even that time-honoured institution, the daily school assembly, my experience of which in all the schools where I was a teacher tended to induce ennui or irritation, was an enlivening occasion. Again I think that this was so partly because it was well done and partly because it was an assembly of a socially and academically homogeneous school. The hymn singing, like the performances of the orchestra, reflected in the first instance the firm insistence of the music master. Before long, however, it developed a momentum of its own. From time to time the older boys whose hymn books contained not merely the words or the music of the melody but all four parts, and whose place in the assembly was in the gallery at the back of the hall, would produce an upsurge of harmony redolent of more festive occasions. The Headmaster helped to sustain the mood by avoiding verbose harangues. His departure from the platform and the signal for an orderly dismissal was marked for us precisely by his putting on his mortar board.

There was no disaffected element among the pupils, no bullying, no stealing, no need to guard one's belongings by carrying them around all day in an outsize brief case, no danger or injury from a bike with brakes malevolently disconnected, no arguing with the referee or foul language in the scrum: nothing in short that portended the sleazy mores of the large post-war secondary school.